ALLEN COUNTY PUBLIC LIBRARY

3 1833 04 39 61 8

2/05

P9-ECS-886

THE USBORNE BOOK OF
SCIENTISTS

Struan Reid
and Patricia Fara

Designed by Russell Punter

Illustrated by Stephen Conlin
and Peter Dennis

Series editor: Anthony Marks

With thanks to Tom Petersen
and Jane Chisholm

Contents

Introduction

This book is about the lives and work of some of the world's greatest scientists, from the earliest observations of the skies to modern theories of the universe. It is not a comprehensive history of science, but it describes in detail the breakthroughs and discoveries that have had the greatest impact on the lives of people through the ages.

What is a scientist?

Scientists are people who gather knowledge about the world and how it works. To do this they ask questions, then try to answer them by using observation and experiment. Today there are many different types of scientist, but until about 200 years ago people did not distinguish between the scientific disciplines. In fact, the word "scientist" was not invented before 1830.

For thousands of years most people believed that the earth lay in the middle of the universe, as this 16th-century engraving shows.

How science began

Science began as a search for knowledge that arose out of a need for survival. For example, early hunters studied the habits and variety of animals they hunted. They discovered the uses of plants and herbs as food and medicine, and worked out how to make use of natural substances such as metals and minerals. By experimenting with these materials, people developed ways to improve the quality of their lives.

16th-century illustration showing liquids being heated and collected in bottles

Today we depend upon science for many of the things we take for granted, for comfort, health and entertainment. This book is about many of the people who made these scientific developments possible.

Expanding frontiers

Scientific knowledge is always expanding, and the scientific truths of one age are often questioned by people of the next. Scientists today generally accept that their theories will be revised in the future. New inventions and discoveries also change the way we look at the world. For example, many 15th-century Europeans believed that the sky was made up of crystal spheres which carried the stars and planets around the earth. But discoveries such as those made possible by the invention of the telescope forced people to reject that idea. They began to regard the universe as larger than had previously been thought. This in turn altered people's ideas of their own position in the universe.

A map of our galaxy formed from radio waves

Historical arrangement

This book is arranged historically, beginning with the earliest scientific ideas and medical skills used in the ancient world. It then considers medieval Arab thinkers and the vital role they played in preserving and developing classical learning and passing it on to Renaissance Europe. From this point on, the book reveals the gradual development of science into the individual disciplines familiar to us today. It discusses the changing relationship between science and religion, and the difficulties that many earlier scientists faced. There are also pages on scientific societies and the very important but underrated role of women scientists. A chart on pages 46-47 outlines the main events described in the book.

Dates

Some of the dates are from the period before the birth of Christ. They are indicated by the letters B.C. Early dates in the period after Christ's birth are indicated by the letters A.D. Some of the dates begin with the abbreviation "c". This stands for *circa*, the Latin for "about". It is used when historians are unsure exactly when an event took place.

Early scientific ideas

Science is the process of gathering knowledge and answering questions about the world and how it works. Today, science is divided into different branches, such as chemistry and biology. But in ancient times people did not make the distinction between science and other forms of investigation. Many questions that we would now regard as scientific were then given religious or philosophical explanations. Very few early "scientists" are known by name, but we do have evidence of their ideas.

This Egyptian painting depicts the constellations (groups of stars) as gods.

The Ancient Egyptians

One of the first civilizations in the history of the world was that of Ancient Egypt. It began over 5000 years ago and lasted for more than 3000 years. The Egyptians were very practical, and were especially skilled as builders and craftspeople. But they were also great thinkers, with theories and ideas about the world around them.

This wall painting shows an Egyptian surveyor taking measurements.

Egyptian priest-astronomers used the position of the moon and stars like a giant clock, to work out the timing of their religious festivals. This enabled them to calculate when the River Nile would flood each year. This was the most important event in the agricultural year. They also used their knowledge of the stars to work out several calendars. The first calendar to divide the year into 365 days may have been introduced by an Egyptian man called Imhotep (see page 8).

The Mesopotamians

The region of Mesopotamia (now in modern Iraq) was the site of several ancient civilizations, including those of Sumer and Babylon. The Sumerians flourished from about 4000B.C. They were skilled astronomers and mathematicians, and built huge temples called ziggurats.

The Sumerians also devised a system of writing known as cuneiform ("wedge-shaped"). This was the first form of writing in which abstract signs, rather than pictures of objects, were used to represent sounds. The Sumerians also used two counting systems. One was a decimal system based on units of ten. The other was based on units of sixty.

The Babylonian civilization flourished in Mesopotamia for over 1300 years from 1900B.C. Babylonian astronomers made many observations of eclipses, the moon and the planets Venus and Mercury. They named the constellations after their gods and divided the skies into areas. This later formed the basis for Greek astrology.

The Babylonians were able to predict future movements of the planets by consulting detailed lists of planetary motions which they had compiled over many years. The purpose of this work was not to explain the motions, but rather to put together calendars and to make predictions about the future. The Babylonians saw the world as a flat disc floating on the seas. Babylon was ringed by mountains.

A Babylonian stone map of the world, c.600B.C.

Central America

From about 2000B.C., several civilizations grew up in Meso-America (Mexico and parts of Central America). One of the greatest was that of the Mayans (300B.C. to A.D.900). Later civilizations included the Toltecs and Aztecs.

Mayan observatory at Chichen Itza, Mexico

This Aztec stone depicts the stars and planets. The Aztecs (c.1300-1521) adopted the Mayan calendar.

The Mayans divided the world into four "directions", or sections, each associated with a tree and a bird. They believed the world was made up from the back of a giant crocodile lying in a pond.

This is part of a Mayan calendar. The Mayans used dots, dashes and curved lines to indicate dates.

Thales of Miletus (c.624-546B.C.)

A mathematician and astronomer, he taught that water was the main ingredient of all things and that the earth was a disc floating on water. The work of Thales is very significant because he tried to give natural explanations to puzzling phenomena. For example, he said that earthquakes were not caused by the anger of the gods, but by eruptions of hot water in the oceans.

Pythagoras

Pythagoras was born on the island of Samos and became one of the most highly respected of the early Greek philosophers. As a young man he visited Egypt and Babylon, and was greatly influenced by many of the ideas he found there. He became an important religious leader whose followers were known as the Pythagorean Order.

Pythagoras' ideas about the universe were based on his emphasis on the importance of particular numbers and symmetry in everything. Because of their love of beauty and order, he and his followers believed that the planets moved in circles, and that the heavens and earth were spherical. These ideas were still extremely influential 2000 years later.

An Athenian coin depicting Pythagoras (c.560-480B.C.)

The earliest Greek science

Scholars in Ancient Greece were known as philosophers, which means "lovers of knowledge". Apart from the subject we now know as philosophy (the study of ideas), they also studied scientific subjects such as mathematics, biology, astronomy and geography. They carefully collected as much information as possible to help their studies.

Thales of Miletus

The first important place of Greek learning was based in the eastern Mediterranean. One of the most influential philosophers there was Thales, who came from the port of Miletus, which is now in Turkey.

Pythagoras worked out how the size of bells relates to the sounds they make.

PYTACORA

5

Science in Ancient Greece

The people of Ancient Greece used stories about their gods to explain things they found puzzling. For example, the god of the sea, called Poseidon, was also known as "the earth-shaker" because he was thought to cause earthquakes when he was angry. But from the 6th century B.C. some people started to look for more practical explanations of how and why things look and behave as they do. In order to obtain this knowledge, they asked lots of questions and made many observations and calculations about all sorts of things in the world around them.

Greek coin showing Poseidon

The Academy at Athens

Plato is regarded as the founder of western philosophy. He was born in Athens and later studied under another famous philosopher called Socrates. When he was in his thirties, Plato decided to travel abroad. He visited many of the lands bordering the Mediterranean Sea and met other philosophers.

By the time he returned to Athens in 388B.C., Plato had decided to become a teacher. The following year he founded a school called the Academy which became famous throughout the Greek world. It lasted for over 900 years until it was closed by the Roman emperor Justinian in A.D.529.

Mosaic showing philosophers at the Academy

Plato's work and influence

Plato developed a set of teachings known as the Doctrine of Ideas, which were handed down to us via the Arabs. They were very important for later thinkers because they linked scientific thought with religion and philosophy. Plato argued that everything we detect with our five senses (sight, hearing, taste, smell and touch) is only an outward appearance. He believed that reality is something that we can never observe but only contemplate with our minds. This became one of the foundations of later western thought. Although Plato had a great influence on later philosophers and scientists, today his views are often regarded as a hindrance to modern experimental science. This is because Plato did not encourage experiment, thinking that observation only confused the search for pure theoretical knowledge. For

Plato (427-347B.C.)

example, he believed that the movements of the planets are best understood by the mind, not by accurate observations. He emphasized mathematics as the key to all knowledge but, unlike Archimedes (see below), was not interested in its practical use.

Tutor to Alexander

Aristotle (384-322B.C.) was born in Macedonia in northeastern Greece. His parents died when he was a boy and he was sent by his guardian to study at Plato's Academy. On Plato's death, he left Athens and journeyed for twelve years in Greece and Asia Minor. He returned to Macedonia in 343B.C., and for three years he served as tutor to the young Prince Alexander of Macedonia (later Alexander the Great). After Alexander succeeded his father as king, Aristotle moved back to Athens and set up his own school, the Lyceum.

This fragment of a mosaic shows Alexander in battle.

Illustration from a Greek cup showing students at work

After Alexander's death in 323B.C., Aristotle left Athens for the last time and retired to his estate at Chalcis on the island of Euboea where he died.

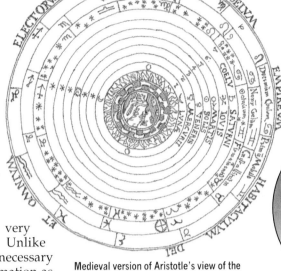

Medieval version of Aristotle's view of the universe

Teaching at the Lyceum

Aristotle's beliefs were very different from Plato's. Unlike Plato, he thought it was necessary to gather as much information as possible. His writings, passed down to us through the ages via the Arabs, laid many of the foundations of modern scientific study.

According to Aristotle, the gods had given a fixed position to every object in the sky above and the earth below. He believed that nothing could change by itself without displacing everything else in the system. Aristotle devised a "Ladder of Nature", with living things placed above inanimate matter such as stones. Human beings were placed above the animals and the gods ruled over them all.

A medieval illustration showing Aristotle's Ladder of Nature

Aristotle believed that the universe consisted of a series of spheres fitting one inside the other, arranged around a spherical earth. Immediately around the earth was the sphere of the atmosphere, followed by spheres containing earth, water, air and fire. Beyond the fire sphere lay a region containing a substance he called the *aether* (from the Greek for "shining"). Farther out still were spheres carrying planets and stars, and finally, around them all, lay a sphere which controlled the movement of the whole system.

Aristotle's influence

Aristotle's main contribution to science was his emphasis on careful observation and very detailed classification. His ideas were highly influential in Europe for about 1500 years. It was not until the Renaissance that they were questioned, most notably by Galileo (see page 18).

Aristotle's system was not in itself rigid. But it was used by many people in the Middle Ages to justify and maintain the feudal system, a strict social order by which kings ruled over lords, who in turn ruled over peasants.

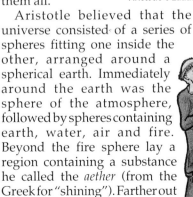

This illustration shows the three main occupations in the Middle Ages: priests, warriors and peasants.

Mathematician and inventor

Archimedes was born in the Greek colony of Syracuse in Sicily. He was a brilliant mathematician and studied at a famous school of learning in Alexandria in Egypt called the Museum. He was killed in 212B.C. when the Romans captured Syracuse.

Archimedes
(287-212B.C.)

He is best known for a law called Archimedes' Principle. This states that when an object is immersed in a fluid it is subject to an upward force equal to the weight of the fluid displaced. It is said that Archimedes shouted *Eureka* ("I have found it") when he saw that his body displaced the water as he climbed into his bath.

Medieval picture of Archimedes in his bath

Practical mathematics

Archimedes used geometry to measure curves and the areas and volumes of solids. He designed leverage systems such as the Archimedean screw for removing water from flooded ships. This principle is still used to raise water from one level to another.

Mosaic showing the murder of Archimedes by a Roman soldier.

Medicine in the ancient world

People have always had to deal with illness, disease and death, but explanations and treatments have varied from area to area throughout history. In many places, illness was seen either as the invasion of the body by some poison or spell, or it was attributed to angry gods who had stolen the person's soul. Early physicians were part doctors and part priests. They believed that medical treatment could relieve the illness, but that the main cause could only be removed by praying to the gods and offering them sacrifices.

Egyptian medicine

The Ancient Egyptians were extremely good surgeons and used a variety of drugs and surgical techniques. Their knowledge of human anatomy was excellent because of their practice of embalming (the preservation of the dead). They believed that the dead person's spirit, or *Ka*, would die if the body rotted away. In order to provide a home for the spirit, the body was preserved as carefully as possible.

This Egyptian wall painting shows part of the embalming process.

First the corpse was cleaned, then the brain and internal organs (such as heart, liver, lungs) were removed and washed in wine. They were then stored in special jars, called canopic jars, with preserving herbs. The body was next

A brightly painted Egyptian canopic jar

stuffed with perfumes and sweet-smelling resins and sewn up. It was covered with natron (a mixture of sodium salts that absorbed moisture) and dried for about 35 days. Finally it was coated with resin, wrapped in linen and placed in an airtight coffin. The most famous Egyptian doctor was called Imhotep (lived c. 2650B.C.). He was also an architect and high priest.

Imhotep

Indian medicine

The best-known ancient Indian medical text is the *Ayurveda*, originally compiled in India around 700B.C. In it, disease is seen as an imbalance of substances in the body. Doctors used medicines to drive out harmful substances, and replace them with ones that were more in tune with the body. The *Ayurveda* also shows that Hindu doctors had a good understanding of diet and the digestive system.

The Ancient Indians excelled in surgical treatment, and the *Ayurveda* describes many different types of surgical instrument. Their doctors knew how to perform many operations, especially on the stomach and bladder. They could also remove cataracts (clouded lenses) from eyes, and were famous for their plastic surgery (rebuilding wounded parts of the body). They used hairs to stitch up torn lips.

An Indian illustration showing a type of plastic surgery of the nose.

Chinese medicine

In the 6th century B.C., a Chinese philosopher called Confucius (551-479B.C.) taught that people are closely linked to a universe dominated by two opposing types of force known as *yin* and *yang*. Yin was regarded as a negative force, while *yang* was positive. He claimed that the harmony of the universe and the health of people depended on keeping a balance between the two forces. Today, many Chinese believe that these two forces circulate around the body in the form of spirits or fluids.

Chinese illustration showing how to take a patient's pulse

By inserting needles at specified points on the body, the correct flow of the two spirits can be maintained. This technique, known as acupuncture, is used to ease the pain of surgical operations instead of drugs. Today in China, and increasingly in the West, acupuncture and other alternative medicines are used with drugs and surgery.

A 17th-century Chinese wooden acupuncture figure

Greek medicine

In the 5th century B.C. a medical school on the small Greek island of Cos became very influential. The physicians at Cos were good at treating bone injuries but knew little about internal organs. They believed that disease was caused by a lack of balance in the body between four fluids - which consisted of blood, black bile, yellow bile and phlegm - and four related qualities - heat, cold, dryness and dampness.

The island was the home of Hippocrates, a doctor who is often known as "the father of medicine". Like modern doctors, he insisted on keeping medical records, noting when treatments failed, as well as when they were successful.

A 14th-century portrait of Hippocrates (c.450-370B.C.)

Hippocrates emphasized the importance of letting the body heal naturally, so he used few drugs, instead recommending treatments such as warm relaxing baths and a simple diet. At that time many people thought that an illness such as epilepsy was a punishment from the gods. But Hippocrates rejected

This medieval illustration shows a Greek patient being treated for a dislocated arm.

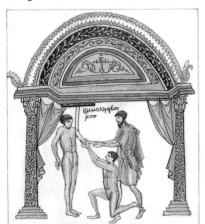

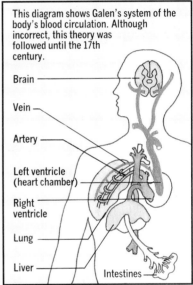

A selection of 2nd-century B.C. Greek surgical instruments

this, and suggested instead that it had natural causes.

Greek medicine was very influential in medieval and Renaissance Europe. Hippocrates' teachings were gathered by Greek scholars to form a massive medical work called the Hippocratic Collection. Parts of it were still being used as textbooks in European medical schools as late as the 19th century. Today, doctors make a promise to work for the benefit of the patient at all times. It is known as the Hippocratic Oath, after Hippocrates.

Roman medicine

The most famous of all doctors in Roman times was Galen. He was born at Pergamum in Asia Minor (now in Turkey) the son of a Greek architect. In A.D.161 he moved to Rome, where he spent nearly all his active life. He set up a medical practice and became so successful that he was eventually appointed physician to the emperor's family.

Galen's work dominated medieval medical thought in the Arabic world and Europe. He did important research into the physical structure and functions of the body. He could not learn anatomy by cutting up dead humans, as this was illegal, and had to use carcasses of apes and pigs. But because animals are different from humans, his anatomical theories contained many errors which were accepted until the work of Vesalius in the 16th century (see page 16).

Bust of Galen (c.A.D.129-200)

Galen's system was wrong in several ways. He put veins (carrying blood to the heart) on the right side of the body and arteries (carrying blood from the heart to various parts of the body) on the left. He believed that blood seeped through pores in the septum (internal wall) of the heart.

This diagram shows Galen's system of the body's blood circulation. Although incorrect, this theory was followed until the 17th century.

Brain

Vein

Artery

Left ventricle (heart chamber)

Right ventricle

Lung

Liver

Intestines

Galen taught that the heart pumped blood through the arteries mixed with something he called "pneuma" (a sort of spirit which the lungs obtain when air is breathed in). He proposed that the blood was sent to the organs that needed it, but not in a circulatory motion. This theory is incorrect, but it was not until the 17th century that an English doctor called William Harvey (see page 17) correctly worked out how the blood circulates continuously all the way around the body.

Islamic science

3 1833 04039 461 8

In Arabia in the 7th century A.D., the Prophet Mohammed founded a new religion called Islam. Within a century of his death in 632, his followers (known as Muslims) had conquered a huge empire that stretched from Spain to the borders of China. The arts and sciences flourished in the Arab world, particularly between 900 and 1200. As well as making their own contributions to science, the Arabs absorbed scientific ideas from many different parts of their great empire, particularly from the Greeks and Persians. In this way Islamic thinkers helped to transmit the ideas of the ancient world to medieval Europeans. Without them, much of this information would have been lost.

This Islamic illustration shows the Greek philosopher Aristotle (see page 6) with a student.

A great thinker

Ibn Sina, known in Europe as Avicenna, was an extremely learned and versatile man who wrote about 270 books on a huge range of subjects. He was born at Bokhara in Iran. At the age of only 16 he was working in medicine. At various times during his life he was a lawyer and teacher of science. He was also involved in politics and acted as adviser to the Iranian ruler. He died of colic

Ibn Sina (980-1037) teaching a class of students

An Islamic manuscript showing a dentist extracting a tooth

(inflammation of the abdomen), but there were suspicions that he may have been poisoned.

Ibn Sina wrote the *Canon*, a huge book about medicine. This work influenced medical teaching in Europe until the 17th century. Islamic law forbade the dissection of the human body, so the book was mainly about how to recognize and treat diseases, and how to prepare drugs. Another of ibn Sina's major works was a large encyclopedia entitled *The Cure*, which covered a wide range of subjects from philosophy to mathematics and physics.

The master of alchemy

Alchemy was a very important part of Arabic thinking. Alchemists mainly looked for a way of changing non precious metals such as iron into gold. Alchemical studies were important because although they used magic and spells, they also involved the use of experiment. This laid the foundations for several modern sciences, including chemistry and mineralogy (the study of minerals).

An alembic, a vessel used in distillation

Al-Razi (c.854-935), known in medieval Europe as Rhazes, was born at Rayy in Iran. He was the greatest Muslim alchemist and one of the most famous figures in medicine of the 9th and 10th

centuries. But al-Razi also questioned religious teachings, and so made himself unpopular with the powerful clergy.

Al-Razi devoted the first part of his life to alchemy. He rejected much of the magic and spells performed by alchemists and concentrated more on their experimental ideas. He was very interested in the use of chemical substances and clearly described some of the techniques used in alchemy, such as distillation (boiling a liquid until it becomes gaseous, then cooling it back into a liquid again).

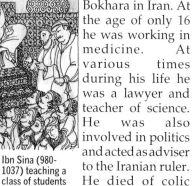

These brass instruments were used in geomancy, a method of prophesying the future.

He also made some of the earliest suggestions for equipping a laboratory, listing some of the instruments.

Al-Razi was appointed director of the hospital in Rayy and then moved to become director of the hospital in Baghdad. He was one of the first of the Muslim writers on medicine, producing over a hundred works on the subject. His most famous publication was the huge *Comprehensive Book* which covered the whole of medical practice known at that time, including Greek, Indian and Chinese medical knowledge.

Islamic surgical instruments

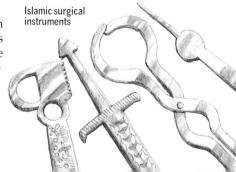

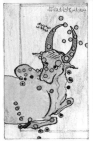

Islamic astrological signs. From left to right: Aries, Taurus, Gemini, Cancer, Leo, Virgo.

Astronomer and courtier

Abu Rayhan al-Biruni (973-c.1050) was born in Khwarazm, Armenia. He began his scientific studies while still very young and by the age of 17 had designed and made an instrument for observing the sun. But in 995 a civil war forced him to flee abroad.

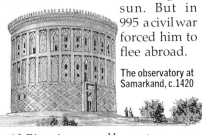

The observatory at Samarkand, c.1420

Al-Biruni returned home two years later and held a number of official positions at royal courts. He continued his scientific studies and astronomical observations, and designed and built many instruments for observing the sun, the moon and the stars.

This Turkish astronomer is observing a meteor with an instrument called a quadrant.

But al-Biruni's interests and studies were not limited to astronomy. In all, he wrote about 13,000 pages of highly technical material about geography, mathematics, optics (the study of light and the eye), medicines and drugs, precious stones and astrology. His interest in alchemy also led him to study the composition of minerals and metals, and his writings in this field later proved very influential as the science of chemistry developed. He also wrote a huge work on mineralogy called *The Book of the Multitude of Knowledge of Precious Stones*. Although he was ill for many years, by the time of his death at the age of 80 he had written over 140 books on many different subjects.

A page from an Islamic book about mineralogy

Lenses and light

Ibn al-Haytham (965-c.1040) was the greatest of all the Islamic physicists. He was born at Basra in Iraq and became known in Europe as Alhazen. He moved to Cairo where he worked at a school called the Academy during the reign of the Caliph al-Hakim (996-1020).

Al-Haytham wrote on a range of subjects, including optics, astronomy and mathematics. His work on optics was so extensive and detailed that it formed the basis of many later European studies of the subject. In his book called *The Treasury of Optics* he rejected an earlier Greek idea that the eye sends out rays of light to the object it is looking at. Instead he suggested that rays of light come from the object to the eye.

A 16th-century illustration of al-Haytham's study of the structure of the eye

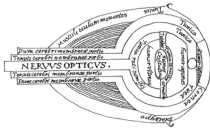

Al-Haytham also examined the effect of light through lenses. He concluded that the refraction (bending) of light is caused by light rays moving at different speeds through different materials, such as air, glass and water. This idea was used in the 17th century by Kepler (see page 15) and Descartes (page 19). Al-Haytham was also the first person to develop the *camera obscura*, a box in which images from outside are projected onto a wall. He used a hole in a wall to reproduce the image of the sun during an eclipse.

A 19th-century English camera obscura, based on al-Haytham's principles.

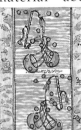
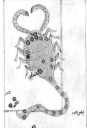

Islamic astrological signs. From left to right: Libra, Scorpio, Sagittarius, Capricorn, Aquarius, Pisces.

Science in medieval Europe

The period from about A.D.400 to 1400 in Europe is often known as the medieval age. For much of this time the Christian Church was very powerful and ruled all aspects of life. As most scholars were Christian monks, they had to follow the teachings of the Church. People who contradicted the Church's views were often persecuted.

From the end of the 11th century, many ancient Greek, Roman and Arab books reached northern Europe through Muslim Spain (see page 10).

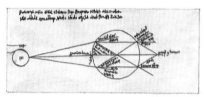

Pope Innocent III (1198-1216), a very powerful Church leader

Bishops feared that the new knowledge contained in these books would make people question the Bible's account of the creation of the world. Over the years, however, much science and philosophy from the classical and Arab worlds was slowly reconciled with Christian teachings.

Religion and philosophy

Thomas Aquinas was an Italian monk. In 1264 he wrote a book, *Summa contra gentiles*, in which he stated that while everything was created by God, knowledge and truth could also come from other sources. He said that on religious questions the Church and the Bible were the only authorities, but that in scientific matters the work of the Greeks and Arabs could also help to explain the world that God had created. These ideas enabled the Church to come to terms with the teachings of the ancient world.

Thomas Aquinas (1225-74)

The rise of new learning

From the late 12th century, places of learning called universities were founded all over Europe. The most important were those at Bologna, Oxford, Cambridge and Paris. Many of the people who taught and studied there were associated with the Church, so the universities became important in developing ideas about religious matters.

Illustration showing man at the middle of the universe which is embraced by God

Robert Grosseteste (c.1168-1253) was born in Sussex, England. He became a leading figure in scientific studies in the first half of the 13th century. He studied at Oxford University and then, from 1209, taught at the University of Paris. In 1214 he returned to Oxford, where he acted as tutor to some of the students, including a community of monks.

A class in progress at the new university at Bologna in Italy.

A supporter of Aristotle

Grosseteste always stressed the great importance of testing all scientific propositions. In this he was a supporter of Aristotle who recommended the use of careful observation and analysis. He wrote on a wide range of subjects, including astronomy and music. His most famous work was on optics and how light behaves, and in this he was influenced by the work of the Arabic scientist ibn al-Haytham (see page 11).

Grosseteste's drawing of light passing through a lens

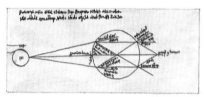

Grosseteste's pupil

Roger Bacon (c.1214-c.1294) was born in Somerset, England. He studied at Oxford University and in 1241 moved to Paris. In 1247 he returned to Oxford where he was one of Grosseteste's pupils. He taught for the rest of his life in England and France.

Bacon did not experiment himself, but he did carry out some research into optics and the eye. He described ibn al-Haytham's account of the eye as a device for forming images. He also understood the causes of the refraction (bending) of light and was one of the first people to suggest that lenses could be used as spectacles for magnification.

This illustration of 1352 is the earliest known picture of lenses being used as spectacles.

Conflict with the Church

When he was almost 40, Bacon became a Franciscan monk. He had an argumentative nature and had many disputes over astronomy and astrology with John of Fidanza (later Saint Bonaventure), the head of the Franciscans.

In 1267, at the invitation of his friend Pope Clement IV, Bacon wrote a work called *Opus majus*, an important volume of papers covering all areas of knowledge. In addition, it condemned the teaching methods of both the Franciscans and the Dominicans, claiming that they were out of date and narrow-minded. This made him still more unpopular with the authorities and even the Pope was outraged. In 1277 Bacon was put on trial and sent to prison in Paris for several years. The charge was that he regarded reason and philosophy as more important than the established teachings of the Christian Church.

Science supporting religion

Bacon is a major figure in the history of science, not because he challenged the authority of the Church, but because of his scientific approach. He believed that the study and advancement of science could complement and support religion. He thought that scientific study would enable people to understand all aspects of the world. In this way, he argued, they would gain a better knowledge of God and his works.

This medieval illustration shows the Church (at the top) controlling the different areas of knowledge (below).

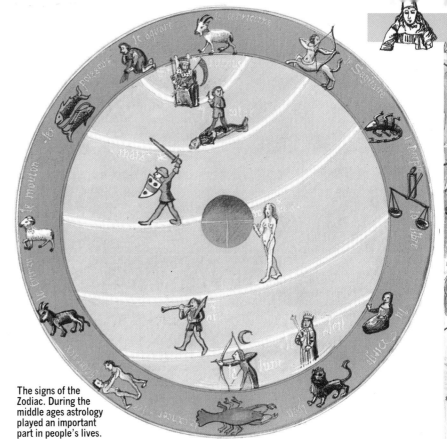

The signs of the Zodiac. During the middle ages astrology played an important part in people's lives.

Aristotle's work is questioned

By the 14th century scholars had adopted many ancient ideas, especially Aristotle's. But they interpreted these rigidly, taking them to mean that the universe was unchanging and perfect, with the earth fixed at the middle.

Jean Buridan (c.1300-85), a teacher at Paris University, adopted a Greek idea called the "impetus theory". His version stated that God had set the planets and stars moving around the earth at a speed that would continue forever. This was an important step toward a physical explanation of planetary motion, because it rejected supernatural causes. Buridan was afraid to publish his work because it contradicted Aristotle's teaching that divine beings pushed the planets along.

The friend of princes

Nicolas Oresme (c.1320-82) was born in Normandy in France and became Bishop of Lisieux. From about 1340 he studied in Paris under Buridan. Oresme went much farther than Buridan in questioning Aristotle's work. He suggested that the earth might not be fixed but might actually rotate daily on its own axis. He also used mathematics to work out planetary movements. Oresme's ideas helped later scientists to formulate new ideas about the structure of the universe. This eventually led to the overthrow of the Aristotelian system by Galileo and others in the 17th century (see page 18).

This medieval engraving depicts a mathematics class.

The earth and the sun

From the earliest times, people have wanted to understand the mystery of the stars and planets. Early civilizations charted the movements of the sun and the moon to construct calendars.

This picture shows Nut, Egyptian goddess of the sky, bending over gods of the earth and air.

The Ancient Egyptians arranged the stars into groups called constellations, which they often gave religious significance. The science of astronomy developed as people gradually learned more about the world beyond them. Astronomers examine the skies in order to answer questions about space and the movements of the planets and stars.

The Ptolemaic system

In about A.D.150 Ptolemy, a Greek astronomer living in Alexandria in Egypt, wrote an important textbook now known as the *Almagest* (Arabic for "the greatest work"). In this, he described a system of the universe in which the earth lay stationary and the moon, the sun, and the planets all moved around it in circular paths called orbits. All the stars were fixed to the surface of a rotating sphere. This idea, which was based on the work of Aristotle (see page 6), is known as the geocentric (from the Greek for earth) theory. It

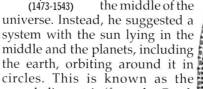

This brass sphere, based on Ptolemy's ideas, was used to work out the positions of the stars.

became the accepted view of the universe for nearly 1400 years. But as new and more efficient instruments were invented to examine the skies, the findings of astronomers became more and more accurate. The new evidence began to contradict Ptolemy's geocentric theory.

Ptolemy (c.A.D.90-170) as shown in this medieval engraving

Doubts are raised

Niklas Kopernik was a Polish monk more commonly known by his latinized name of Copernicus. He studied mathematics, medicine and law in Poland and Italy and became a canon at Frauenburg Cathedral in Poland. There he became interested in astronomy, and he began to doubt that the earth lay at the middle of the universe. Instead, he suggested a

Copernicus (1473-1543)

system with the sun lying in the middle and the planets, including the earth, orbiting around it in circles. This is known as the heliocentric (from the Greek for sun) theory.

Copernicus recorded this theory in a book called *De revolutionibus orbium caelestium* ("Concerning the revolutions of the heavenly spheres").

The Church, however, taught that the earth was the heart of the universe, which was the view that had been presented in the Bible. Because

he was a clergyman, Copernicus decided not to publish his book for fear of being criticized and punished by the Church.

In 1543, shortly before he died, Copernicus was finally persuaded to publish his book. But without his knowledge, the publishers added a preface in order to protect themselves from criticism by the Church. It stated that Copernicus' scheme was not a real picture of the universe, but only a theory. This reduced the impact of the book when it came out. But while his book contained many ideas we now know to be incorrect, it provided a structure for the work of such later astronomers as Kepler (see opposite) and Galileo.

Engraving of the Copernican, heliocentric system of the universe

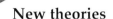

A new star appears

Tycho Brahe was born in Skåne, then in Denmark but now Sweden. He was a very quarrelsome man and had most of his nose cut off in a duel. While studying at Copenhagen University, he became very interested in astronomy.

In 1572 astronomers noticed that a new star had appeared in the sky. (It was probably an exploding object now known as a supernova.) Brahe calculated that the new star lay beyond the moon. This conflicted with the Aristotelian theory that only the skies between the earth and the moon could change.

Brahe's observatory on Hven

An island observatory

In 1574 Brahe set up an observatory on Hven, an island in the Baltic Sea given to him by King Frederick II of Denmark. His observations of a comet (see page 23) in 1577 showed that it moved among the planets lying beyond the moon. This again proved that changes did occur in the skies. Although his findings contradicted Aristotle's view of the universe on several fundamental points, Brahe would not accept Copernicus' view because it opposed the teachings of the Church. Instead he proposed a compromise, a system in which the planets orbited the sun, and the sun orbited the earth, which lay still at the heart of the universe.

When Frederick died in 1588, the Danish royal family withdrew the money used for the upkeep of the Hven observatory. The following year Brahe moved to Prague. He remained there for the rest of his life, continuing his work as an astronomer.

A contemporary drawing of the 1572 supernova

Tycho Brahe (1546-1601)

Medallion commemorating the great comet of 1577

New theories

Johannes Kepler was born in Germany. He taught mathematics at Graz in Austria, then moved to Prague to become Brahe's assistant. When Brahe died he left his astronomical findings to Kepler, instructing him to use them to disprove Copernicus' theories.

Kepler worked for years on the orbits of the planets, but the information he had collected did not fit with the theories of either Brahe or Copernicus. He worked out that although the planets did indeed circle around the sun, they moved not in perfect circles but in extended circular paths called ellipses. He also realized that the speed of the planets varies as they travel, according to their distance from the sun. These ideas are the basis of Kepler's three laws of planetary movement. He also understood that the sun has a very strong influence on the movement of the planets.

Johannes Kepler (1571-1630)

Kepler published many of his theories in his books *The New Astronomy* (1609) and *Epitome of Copernican Astronomy* (1621). At the time most people did not realize the significance of his ideas, but his writings influenced many later scientists. Newton used Kepler's laws when he formulated his theories of gravity (see page 22).

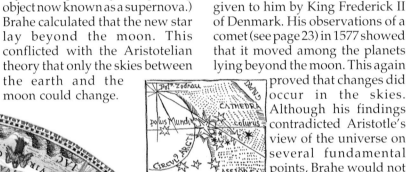

Understanding the human body

During the Middle Ages medical knowledge in Europe remained based on the work of Galen and other early doctors (see pages 8-9). In the 12th century, however, new ideas began reaching western Europe, as Greek and Arab medical texts were translated into Latin. Doctors and medical scientists began to question ancient theories and later to replace them with new ones of their own.

A flamboyant personality

Aureolus Philippus Theophrastus Bombastus von Hohenheim, otherwise known as Paracelsus, was born near Zürich in Switzerland. He studied at the University of Ferrara in Italy, then worked as a surgeon in the army. Paracelsus was a violent man who angered even his closest friends. He charged rich people huge fees, but treated the poor for free. He took the name Paracelsus because he disagreed so much with the Roman physician Celsus and other traditional doctors. (*Para* is the Greek word for "beyond" or "against".)

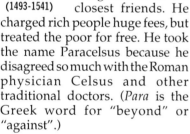
Paracelsus (1493-1541)

A restless doctor

In 1527 Paracelsus became professor of medicine at Basle University, where he also had a successful doctor's practice. But he had many arguments with the

16th-century illustration showing Paracelsus lecturing

medical authorities and, after publicly burning books by Galen and Avicenna, he had to leave Basle. For the rest of his life he journeyed around Europe, never staying more than two years in one place, and died in Austria.

This picture shows Paracelsus performing a surgical operation.

Paracelsus did not believe in the old Greek idea that disease was caused by an imbalance of the four fluids (see page 9). Instead he thought it was caused by a poison entering the body. He sometimes treated people with drugs that produced symptoms similar to those of the disease they had. This was an early form of homeopathy, a method that claims to heal the body by reinforcing its natural defences.

The great anatomist

Andreas Vesalius was born in Brussels, the son of an apothecary (pharmacist) to the Holy Roman Emperor, Charles V. He first studied at Louvain (now in Belgium), then at the University of Paris, but war forced him back to Louvain. By this time Vesalius was very interested in human anatomy, the science of the structure of the body. In order to study this thoroughly, he needed to dissect (cut up) dead bodies. As this was forbidden by law, he sometimes had to rob graves to get the corpses he required, or take the bodies down from gallows. In 1537 he attended the medical school at Padua in Italy,

one of the most famous in Europe. His knowledge was already so extensive that he was awarded his doctorate after only two days of exams, then appointed lecturer of anatomy. He later became physician to Charles V, but in 1564 he drowned in a shipwreck on his way back to Madrid from a pilgrimage to Jerusalem.

Galen's work is questioned

While he was at Padua, Vesalius carried out as many dissections as possible, using animals as well as human bodies. He did all the dissections himself and used large anatomical diagrams as guides for his students. But these drawings were still based on Galen's theories.

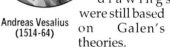
Andreas Vesalius (1514-64)

Vesalius gradually discovered many differences between Galen's ideas and the results of his own dissections. By 1539 he was able to prove that Galen's descriptions fitted an ape's body rather than a human being's. In 1543 he published *The Fabric of the Human Body*, one of the greatest scientific books ever written. It gave anatomy the status of an academic pursuit, and by the 17th century Vesalius' theories were accepted almost everywhere in Europe.

A drawing from *The Fabric of the Human Body*

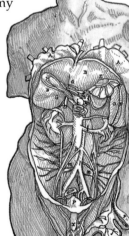

This illustration from *The Fabric of the Human Body* shows the body's muscles.

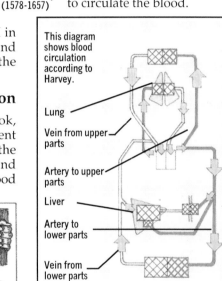

A royal physician

William Harvey was born in Folkestone, England. After studying arts and medicine at Cambridge University, he went to Padua to continue his medical training with a famous professor of anatomy called Fabricius. In 1602 he returned to London and set up a medical practice. He was appointed physician at St Bartholomew's Hospital, London in 1609. In 1618, he was made physician to James I in 1618, and later to Charles I, and was a staunch royalist during the English Civil War.

William Harvey
(1578-1657)

A new theory of circulation

In 1628 Harvey published a book, *De motu cordis* ("On the movement of the heart and blood"). It was the product of many observations and set out his theories about how blood travels around the body.

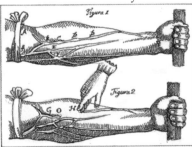

Harvey's diagram showing valves in the veins

At that time, most doctors believed Galen's idea that blood was passed from one side of the heart to the other through small holes. From his own experiments, Harvey introduced the concept of circulation, showing that blood flows away from the heart through the arteries, and back to the heart through veins. Fabricius had found valves in the veins, but had not understood their function.

Harvey realized that the valves in large veins direct the blood back toward the heart, and that the valves of the heart keep the blood flowing around the body in one direction only - to the lungs from the right side, and to the rest of the body from the left. He also realized that the heart acts as a pump to circulate the blood.

This diagram shows blood circulation according to Harvey.

Lung

Vein from upper parts

Artery to upper parts

Liver

Artery to lower parts

Vein from lower parts

One more puzzle

Harvey's discovery was a brilliant piece of reasoning based on observation. But there was still a final question: how did blood that left the heart through the arteries enter the veins? Harvey guessed that tiny blood vessels must connect the veins and arteries, but he was unable to prove it. In 1661, while examining a frog's lungs under a microscope, an Italian called Marcello Malpighi (1628-94) found the tiny linking vessels (called capillaries) and the puzzle was finally solved.

17

Science during the Renaissance

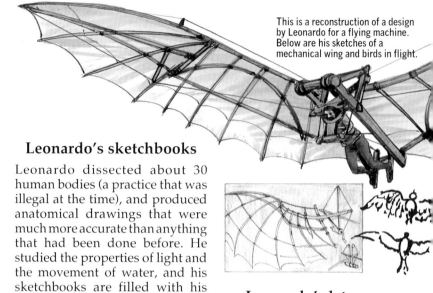

This is a reconstruction of a design by Leonardo for a flying machine. Below are his sketches of a mechanical wing and birds in flight.

I n Europe in the 14th century there began a period of about 200 years that became known as the Renaissance (meaning "rebirth"). During this time people began to rediscover the arts and learning of Ancient Greece and Rome, and to develop new ideas about the world around them. They began to look at things more critically and observation and experiment in all areas became more important. They also challenged the established Aristotelian teachings, which combined Greek and Christian philosophy (see page 12).

The universal man

Many thinkers during the Renaissance believed in the ideal of the "universal man", someone who combined a wide range of talents and interests. Leonardo da Vinci was a painter, sculptor, musician, architect, scientist and an ingenious inventor who typified this ideal.

Leonardo da Vinci (1452-1519)

Leonardo was born near Florence, the son of a legal clerk called Pietro da Vinci. His father noticed Leonardo's artistic talents and sent him to work in the studio of a painter called Andrea del Verrochio. Although he only completed a relatively small number of paintings, Leonardo is now recognized as one of the world's greatest artists. One of his most famous pictures is the *Mona Lisa*, which he painted in 1503.

Leonardo's sketchbooks

Leonardo dissected about 30 human bodies (a practice that was illegal at the time), and produced anatomical drawings that were much more accurate than anything that had been done before. He studied the properties of light and the movement of water, and his sketchbooks are filled with his designs for mechanical devices, including flying machines. We now know that many of these would not have worked, but they demonstrate Leonardo's ability to combine detailed observation with powerful imagination.

Sketches by Leonardo showing various anatomical features

Leonardo's later years

From 1483 Leonardo worked in Milan as an inspector of fortifications, and then in Florence as a military engineer. In 1507 he moved to Amboise in France, where he spent the rest of his life.

Despite his enormous range and creativity, Leonardo's work had little influence on the progress of science. His studies were made for his own satisfaction; most of his contemporaries knew nothing of them. His many sketches and notebooks were dispersed after his death and remained largely unknown for centuries.

Copernicus' champion

Galileo Galilei (1564-1642) was born in Pisa in Italy, the son of a composer. He played a vital part in establishing Copernicus' view (see page 14) that the earth rotates around a stationary sun. A pioneer of the experimental approach to science which was developing at this time, he was also a gifted teacher.

At the age of 17, Galileo enrolled as a medical student at the University of Pisa.

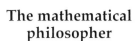

While he was attending a service at the cathedral, he noticed that the chandeliers were swinging in a wind, and used his pulse to time their movements. He found that though the swings slowly got smaller they always took the same amount of time. This led him to suggest that pendulums could be used to measure time. This idea was the basis of the first mechanical clocks.

Galileo left Pisa to continue his work in mechanics and mathematics, but he later returned there as professor of mathematics. The results of his experiments at this time provided increasing evidence to contradict many of Aristotle's theories about the organization of the universe (see page 6).

"And yet it moves!"

After hearing about the invention of the telescope in Holland, Galileo designed and built some more powerful models himself. In 1610 he published his observations of the stars and planets in *The Starry Messenger*, a book which became both popular and influential. In it he described mountains on the moon, and dark spots which occasionally move across the face of the sun. He also showed that some planets, like Jupiter, have their own small orbiting planets. Galileo's work demonstrated the uses of the telescope. But more importantly, all his findings supported the view of Copernicus that the earth rotates around the sun.

Two of Galileo's telescopes

In 1632 Galileo published his *Dialogue Concerning the Two Chief World Systems*, which summed up his observations. The work was seen as a masterpiece all over Europe. But in Italy it clashed with the teachings of the Church, which upheld the traditional view of the earth lying in the middle of the solar system.

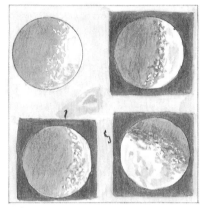

Paintings by Galileo of the surface of the moon

In 1633 Galileo was charged with heresy (holding a view contrary to the established teaching of the Church). He was brought before a Church court in Rome known as the Inquisition. Having been found guilty, he was threatened with torture unless he publicly denied his claim that the earth moved round the sun. Appearing old and frail, Galileo did as the Inquisition demanded. He was ordered to retire to the countryside for the rest of his life. But it is said that as he was leaving the court he murmured "And yet it moves!" because he still believed in his theory.

Galileo's sketch of the method of measuring the height of mountains on the moon

The mathematical philosopher

The ideas of René Descartes were very influential in both mathematics and philosophy. He was born in Brittany in France, the son of a lawyer. In 1628 he moved to the Netherlands, where the Protestant Church took a more relaxed view of new ideas. He worked there for the next 20 years.

One of the most important contributions Descartes made to philosophy was his concept of doubt. He did not accept an unquestioning belief in biblical and classical sources of knowledge. He declared that his own existence was the only thing he could be certain about: *Cogito ergo sum* ("I think, therefore I am"). In his major scientific work, *Principles of Philosophy*, he suggested that the movement of the universe could be described in terms of moving particles of various sizes.

René Descartes (1596-1650)

Drawing by Descartes which shows the universe as whirlpools of matter

Descartes laid the basis for co-ordinate mathematics, a system that enables different quantities, such as age and height, to be related to each other in graphs or charts. His ideas on the structure of the universe were very influential, though they were later challenged by Newton (see page 22).

Scientific societies

In Europe from the middle of the 17th century, groups of men began to meet regularly in such cities as London, Florence, Oxford and Paris to discuss their scientific experiments and ideas. They were mostly wealthy people who experimented at home and who wanted to share their discoveries. These very informal meetings developed into the first scientific societies. During the following centuries, these societies grew stronger and more influential, often helped by an increasing government interest in science. Partly as a result of their influence, science gradually divided into specialized subjects such as geology and astronomy, and many people began to take up the activity of scientific research as a paid career.

Part of the Charter of the Royal Society, granted by Charles II

would lead to new scientific discoveries and enable people to develop new theories. He suggested that scientists should collect facts and figures on each subject and from as many sources as possible. In 1627 he published *The New Atlantis*, his last book. This described his vision of a world in which scientists were dedicated to improving the lives of everyone in the community.

Although Bacon did not carry out any scientific experiments himself, his ideas remained very influential for many years. During the 17th century, his writings and his philosophy of experiment stimulated people all over Europe to establish new scientific organizations.

The coat of arms of the Royal Society, the earliest scientific society

mainly doctors, philosophers, and important officials. They included the architect Christopher Wren and the writer Samuel Pepys. The Royal Society is still in existence today and is an important forum for ideas.

A belief in experiment

Francis Bacon was the son of a courtier to King Henry VIII of England. He trained as a lawyer, eventually becoming a politician under Queen Elizabeth I. In 1617 King James I appointed him Lord Chancellor of England, but in 1621 he was convicted of taking bribes, dismissed from office and banished from the royal court.

Bacon wrote about his views on scientific methods in a series of books and essays. He felt that it was important to find the answers to scientific problems by means of experiment. In his book *Novum organum* he argued that careful experiment and observation

Francis Bacon (1561-1626)

The Royal Society

The establishment of the Royal Society in London was extremely important because for the first time it offered a permanent meeting place for the scientific community. Members were no longer isolated individuals but now felt that they belonged together in a social group where they could discuss their latest experiments.

The Society was founded in 1662, at the beginning of the reign of Charles II. It received the personal backing of the king, who granted it a Royal Charter that outlined its purposes and gave it certain rights. The founding members were

This engraving shows Gresham College, a scientific college founded in 1596 which was a forerunner of the Royal Society.

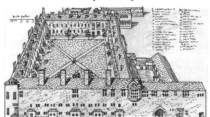

This illustration of Louis XIV visiting the Académie Royale des Sciences was issued by the French government in the 17th century.

Académie Royale des Sciences

The Académie Royale des Sciences was founded in Paris in 1666. Although it was based on the Royal Society, it was very different from its counterpart in England. The French king, Louis XIV, was keen to use science to increase his own power and influence, and he took a close interest in the running of the Académie.

Membership was strictly limited to those people who had proved

A giant burning lens made and used by Lavoisier (see page 30) in experiments at the Académie Royale des Sciences.

themselves to be academically excellent and who also had the king's approval. However, unlike the members of the English Royal Society, who never received a salary, the French academicians were paid by the government. This marked the beginning of the age of the salaried scientist.

The Académie produced a lot of excellent scientific work, especially in the second half of the 18th century. But because of its strong links with the monarchy it was abolished during the French Revolution. It was replaced by the Institut de France, which was founded by Napoleon.

Specialist societies in Britain

Until scientific study became common in universities in the second half of the 19th century, scientists tended to discuss their ideas in learned societies. The members included people from a range of backgrounds, including industry, chemistry and medicine. This interaction of people and skills contributed to the Industrial Revolution, which happened earlier

in Britain than in the rest of Europe. From the end of the 18th century, many countries in Europe were transformed into industrial nations.

Specialist societies grew up in London, such as the Linnean Society (biology and natural history) in 1788, the Geology Society in 1807, and the Astronomical Society in 1831. They quickly became professional organizations with their own journals and limited membership.

Germany in the 19th century

Justus von Liebig was one of the greatest chemists of the 19th century. He was born in Germany, the son of a chemist. In 1822 he moved to Paris to study chemistry. He visited laboratories in France and was very impressed by the standards of chemistry he found there. On his return to Germany he set up his own research laboratory in 1824 at the University of Giessen. Here teamwork rather than individual research was encouraged.

Justus von Liebig (1803-73)

Liebig's laboratory was one of the best equipped in Europe. (He invented the Liebig condenser, a cooling device that turns gases into liquids.) His work influenced the development of Germany's industries, particularly those that produced dyes and drugs. In the 19th century German universities became places of scientific research that acted as the models for new universities all over the world.

Bottles of artificial dye, produced in Germany in the 19th century

21

The rise of experiment

Today experimentation is regarded as one of the main activities of scientists, but for many centuries this was not the case. Scientific ideas were often based on religion and philosophy rather than experiment. But at the end of the 17th century scientists began to stress the importance of experiment as a valid way of gaining knowledge. They examined the natural world in a new light, trying out new ideas and instruments. Their methods and achievements were to shape western scientific thinking.

Physicist and mathematician

Isaac Newton, one of the most famous scientists in the world, was born into a farming family in Lincolnshire, England. He went to Cambridge University in 1661 to study mathematics and graduated in 1665, the year of the Great Plague. When the plague spread to Cambridge, the university was closed down and Newton returned to Lincolnshire.

Newton's house in Lincolnshire

Newton went back to Cambridge in 1667 and two years later became professor of mathematics there. He later moved to London, where from 1703 until his death he was President of the Royal Society (see page 20).

Isaac Newton
(1642-1727)

Motion and gravity

Newton's stay in Lincolnshire was very productive, but it was not until 1687 that the material he worked on while he was there was published as a book. The full title, translated from the original Latin, was *The Mathematical Principles of Natural Philosophy*, but it is usually known as the *Principia*.

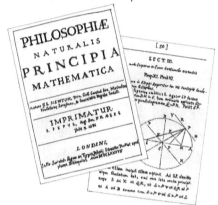

Pages from Newton's book the *Principia*

The first volume included Newton's three Laws of Motion and his theory of gravitation. He is said to have begun wondering about this when he saw an apple fall. He noted that there is a force between the earth and all objects which pulls them together. The earth pulls things like the apple toward it by force of gravity.

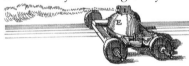

A device designed by Newton to illustrate his Third Law of Motion

With the use of mathematical calculations, Newton was able to solve the age-old problem of how planets move in space. He demonstrated that, in the same way as the apple was pulled to earth, the planets were pulled around the sun by gravitation. This proved Kepler's laws of planetary motion (see page 15), which had been based on observation. Newton brought

the whole of the universe - the earth as well as the stars and planets - under one set of mathematical laws, organized under the principle of universal gravitation. This has had a major influence on scientific thinking up to the present day.

Experiments with light

In 1704 Newton published another famous work, entitled *Opticks*. This described his experiments with light. In one, he directed a beam of sunlight through a glass prism in a dark room. He noticed that the light was split into the different shades of the spectrum, ranging from violet to red.

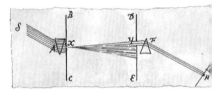

Newton's sketch of his light experiments

Newton's experiment showed that sunlight is not white, but a mixture of violet, indigo, blue, green, yellow, orange and red.

An 18th-century cartoon mocking Newton's Laws of Gravity

Pumps and pressure

Robert Boyle, the fourteenth child of the Earl of Cork, was born at the family's castle in Lismore, Ireland. He went to school in England and then journeyed throughout Europe, accompanied by tutors. There he first read the works of Galileo (see page 18) which had a great influence on him.

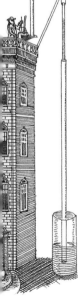

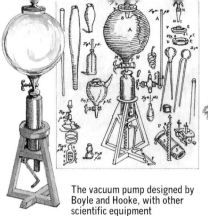

The vacuum pump designed by Boyle and Hooke, with other scientific equipment

In 1654, while at Oxford University, Boyle became interested in investigations being carried out in Europe on the nature of the vacuum. (A vacuum is a closed space from which everything, including air, has been removed.) By 1658, with the help of Robert Hooke (see below), he had designed and built a new kind of air pump. The two scientists used it to create a vacuum by pumping air out of a glass globe. It was used mainly for research into air and air pressure, and to study how animals and plants breathe.

Robert Boyle (1627-91)

An atomic theory of matter

Boyle's work with air and gases enabled him to formulate a law that describes the relationship between the volume of a gas and its pressure. He showed that if an amount of gas is stored at a constant temperature, and the pressure on it is doubled, its volume reduces by half.

This illustration shows one of Boyle's experiments on the pressure of liquids.

In 1661 Boyle published a book called *The Sceptical Chymist*. One of his conclusions was that if air could be compressed it must be made up of tiny particles. He suggested that everything was made up of "primary particles" that could collect together to form larger "corpuscles". He was in fact describing what scientists now call atoms and molecules, though these terms were not introduced until later by Dalton and others (see page 31).

A mechanical genius

Robert Hooke (1635-1703) was an outstanding experimenter and inventor of new instruments. He was born on the Isle of Wight, off the south coast of England. While at Oxford University he met Robert Boyle, who employed him as an assistant.

Hooke moved to London in 1660, and two years later became the curator of

Hooke's compound microscope

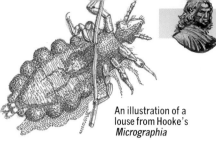

An illustration of a louse from Hooke's *Micrographia*

experiments at the Royal Society. In 1665 he published *Micrographia*, a book containing illustrations of some of the specimens he had viewed under microscopes (instruments which magnify small objects). It also showed several instruments that he had designed. These included the compound microscope which was much more accurate than early microscopes.

The return of a comet

Edmond Halley (1656-1742) was the son of a London businessman. His experimental work in astronomy and magnetism was of great importance. He first became interested in comets (giant balls of ice and dust that move around the solar system) with the appearance of the Great Comet in 1682.

Halley's comet also appeared before the Battle of Hastings in 1066, as shown here (top) in the Bayeux Tapestry.

Applying Newton's theory of gravitation, Halley noted that the orbits of the comets seen in 1531, 1607 and 1682 were very similar and that the comets appeared at regular intervals. He believed that they must all be the same comet and correctly predicted its return in 1758. It is now named after him and its reappearance helped support Newton's picture of the universe.

Classifying the natural world

Ever since people first hunted animals and gathered plants, they have been aware of the great variety of living things. From the earliest times people tried to arrange the different types into groups according to their characteristics, in order to understand them better. This is known as classification. Over the years, however, so many new varieties were discovered and identified that new classification systems were needed to accommodate them.

This is a page from an Arabic version of a classification of animals by Aristotle.

Pages from Gesner's *Historiae animalium*, written between 1551 and 1558

Edward Topsell's *The Historie of Foure-footed Beastes* (above) was the English translation of Gesner's work.

An early naturalist

Konrad Gesner (1516-65) was born in Switzerland. In 1537, at the age of only 21, he was appointed professor of Greek at the newly-founded Lausanne Academy. He eventually worked as a physician in Zürich, and died there in a plague epidemic.

Gesner is famous for the huge five-volume work he compiled entitled *Historiae animalium* (History of animals). In it, he listed alphabetically every creature he could find from his own observations and from books.

Although this work included such mythical creatures as the bishop-fish, it was an important step toward a new understanding of animals. It gave many details of the appearance of the animals, what they ate and where they lived.

Classification takes shape

One of the most outstanding developments in classification was made by John Ray in the 17th century. He was born in Essex, England. His mother was a well-known medical herbalist who encouraged her son's interest in botany. Ray lectured on botany at Cambridge University for more than ten years, but had to leave for religious reasons. He then toured Europe with a biologist called Francis Willughby. After returning to England in 1660, Ray produced a botanical catalogue entitled *Plants Growing in the Neighbourhood of Cambridge*.

John Ray (1627-1705)

Between 1686 and 1704 Ray wrote an enormous book called *A General Account of Plants* which contained descriptions of 17,000 different types. His system of classification of the plants in this work was organized according to their fruits, flowers and leaves. This was an important advance on Gesner's method of classifying animals, which merely listed particular features. Ray's system, however, detailed different features of the plants and then grouped them according to the characteristics they shared. This gave a clearer idea of how they were related to each other.

An illustration from Ray's *Flora of Britain*

Animals from a 17th-century naturalist's museum

Modern classification

The Swedish botanist Carl von Linné is often known by his latinized name of Linnaeus. He studied medicine at the University of Uppsala in Sweden, but spent much of his time there studying plants in the university gardens. Linnaeus then settled at Leiden in the Netherlands for three years. While he was there he published a vast number of works, including *Systema naturae* (System of nature). Two years later he wrote *Genera plantarum* (The Genera of plants).

Linnaeus (1707-78)

Linnaeus worked at Uppsala from 1741 until his death in 1778. He was first appointed professor of medicine, but became professor of botany the following year.

A page from *Systema naturae* by Linnaeus

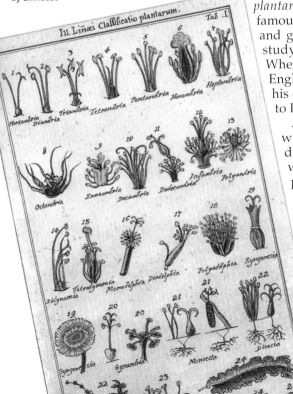

In 1753 Linnaeus published his *Species plantarum*, which is now regarded as the starting point for the modern system of classification of plants. In it he developed a method of classification called "binomial nomenclature" (two-part naming system), a method which is still used in a modified form today.

Linnaeus' house at Uppsala

The binomial system gives each plant two names. The first indicates the genus, or large family group to which it belongs, and the second gives the species, or smaller specific type within the genus. In this way a lemon tree is named *Citrus limon*, while an orange tree is a *Citrus aurantium*.

The publication of *Species plantarum* made Linnaeus famous throughout Europe and greatly influenced the study of natural history. When Linnaeus died, an English admirer shipped his collection and papers to London.

Although Linnaeus was aware of the differences between wild and domesticated plants, he still claimed that the universe had remained the same since God's creation. He regarded each species of plant and animal as fixed and unchanging. This view was challenged by Buffon.

Evidence of change

Georges-Louis Leclerc, Comte de Buffon, was born into a wealthy family living near Dijon, France. He became very active in scientific circles and studied mathematics and botany. In 1739 he was appointed superintendent of the royal botanical garden in Paris, the Jardin du Roi.

Buffon wrote two major works: the *Mémoires* (1737-52), scientific treatises on a range of topics in mathematics, astronomy and physics; and the 36-volume *Natural History* (1749-88). The second book was a survey of the natural world and a history of the Earth. In it, Buffon suggested that fossils provided evidence of extinct species of animal life.

Georges de Buffon (1707-88)

Researchers at the Jardin du Roi

Contradicting Linnaeus, Buffon claimed that fossils showed that the natural world had not remained unaltered, but had changed over the years. The *Natural History* was very important because it was the first book to propose that species had developed over long periods of time. But much more work was needed before the theory of evolution could be devised (see page 28).

Buffon claimed that fossils showed evidence of change.

The age of the earth

Before the 19th century, most theories about the earth and its history were based on biblical accounts. But people gradually began to find evidence that the earth was much older than the Bible suggested. It was discovered that some strata (layers) of rock were older than others, and evidence from fossils indicated many extinct species of plants and animals. Volcanoes and earthquakes showed that the surface of the earth did in fact change. A new science, called geology, developed as people tried to answer questions about how old the earth really is. Geology is the study of the earth's origins, structure and history.

This 16th-century illustration shows God creating the world in six days.

The Neptunist theory

Abraham Werner was born into a wealthy German family with connections in the iron and mining industries. He originally studied law, but later gave this up to study geology. In 1775 at Freiberg in Saxony, Werner founded an institute for studying mining and mineralogy. He worked out the first widely accepted system for classifying types of rock and landscape.

Toward the end of the 18th century many people thought the earth had been shaped by the action of volcanoes and earthquakes. But Werner proposed instead that the earth had once been covered by a huge ocean, created by the flood described in the Bible. This water slowly receded, leaving behind layers of rocks which were formed from minerals in the water. This is known as the "Neptunist" theory, after Neptune, the Roman god of the sea. One of Werner's most important conclusions was that this process must have taken a very long time, as much as one million years. This had a great influence on the work of later geologists.

Abraham Werner (1749-1817)

The Plutonist theory

Although he trained first as a lawyer in Scotland and then qualified as a medical doctor, James Hutton became a famous geologist. In 1795 he published a book called *The Theory of the Earth*. In this he did not include the biblical idea of a flood. Instead he suggested that the earth had changed very slowly over millions of years, and was continuing to do so. According to his theory, the earth's crust was first eroded by natural forces like wind, water, earthquakes and volcanoes. Then the material from this erosion formed a layer and hardened into the earth's surface. Lastly, heat from the middle of the earth caused the movement of rocks, which in turn formed new continents. He suggested that this cycle goes on all the time so that the earth is constantly renewing itself. Hutton's idea is known as the "Plutonist" theory, after Pluto, the Roman god of the underworld. It encouraged a new way of thinking. While Werner's theory had also suggested that the creation of the world took an extremely long time, it could still be related to the flood of the Bible. Hutton's theory, on the other hand, questioned the literal interpretation of the biblical account of the creation.

James Hutton (1726-96) collecting rock samples

This is an early illustration of an eruption of Mt Vesuvius, a volcano in southern Italy.

Fossils

Fossils are the remains of plants and animals preserved in rocks. They are as old as the rocks in which they are found and some were formed more than 500 million years ago. By studying fossils closely, it is possible to build up a picture of life as it was on earth many millions of years ago.

Promicroceras Lower Jurassic

Onnia Ordovician

Uniform change

Charles Lyell was born in Scotland. He studied law at Oxford University, but became interested in geology at the age of 21. In 1831 he was appointed professor of geology at King's College, London. He helped turn the subject from a hobby for rich amateurs into a science in its own right.

Lyell thought that geological features were caused by natural processes acting over very long periods of time. Winds wore away mountains, glaciers moved huge rocks, volcanoes erupted, valleys were eroded by rivers and cliffs by the sea. This theory is known as "uniformitarianism" because it claims that nature acts uniformly in a set pattern. The theory had first been proposed in a general way by Hutton. But it was much more convincingly argued and

Charles Lyell
(1797-1875)

illustrated by Lyell who used new information gathered after Hutton's day to support his ideas. In time it became the view of most geologists and remains so today.

Supercontinents

Alfred Wegener was a German meteorologist (someone who examines weather conditions). He studied at the universities of Berlin, Heidelberg and Innsbruck. In 1910, looking at a map of the world, Wegener noticed that part of the west coast of Africa appeared to fit the shape of the east coast of South America. From this and fossil evidence he suggested that the two continents had once been joined together in one "supercontinent", which he called Pangaea. He then suggested that Pangaea had broken up and that the present continents were formed from the drifting pieces. This is known as the "continental drift" theory.

From 1960 Wegener's ideas were extended to make up the new theory of "plate tectonics". This claims that the earth's crust is not one solid mass, but is cracked into giant pieces (known as "plates")

carrying the continents. The theory describes a never-ending process, in which molten rock is forced up between the plates to the earth's surface, where it solidifies. Similarly, the edges of the plates slide down beneath the adjacent ones and become molten again. If this does not happen and two plates collide, earthquakes occur along the point of impact.

Continental drift

These illustrations show the gradual break-up of Pangaea into the continents we see today.

200 million years ago — Africa / America

65 million years ago — Africa / America

2 million years ago — Africa / America

According to the continental drift theory, the continents of the southern hemisphere once fitted together as one giant continent, as did those of the northern hemisphere. Because the earth's crust has drifted, the continents have not always been in the same place, and are still moving. For example, according to the theory, North Africa was once covered in a sheet of ice and was situated where the South Pole is today. The South Pole was once covered with tropical forests.

Lyell's drawings of fossil shells

Alfred Wegener (1880-1930)

Fossil Chara from the Rockmarl

Isastrea
Middle Jurassic

Evolution

Until the end of the 17th century, most Europeans believed that everything in nature was exactly the same as it always had been; they thought that plant and animal species were fixed, remaining in the state in which they had originally been created by God. In the 18th century, however, an increasing amount of evidence built up which contradicted this. People started to suggest that the characteristics of plants and animals could have changed over very long periods of time. This is now known as evolution.

Early evolutionary ideas

Jean-Baptiste de Monet, Chevalier de Lamarck, was born in France, the eleventh and youngest child of aristocratic but poor parents. He had a difficult life and died poor and blind, his work forgotten. At the age of 16 he joined the army but he had to leave because of ill health. Lack of money forced him to work in a bank rather than taking up his preferred career in medicine.

Chevalier de Lamarck (1744-1829)

Botanist to the king

In his spare time, Lamarck took up the study of plants and became so good at the subject that eventually, in 1781, he was appointed botanist to the French king. Ten years later, after the French Revolution, he was elected professor of zoology at the new Museum of Natural History in Paris. There he gave lectures, arranged the displays and organized exhibitions.

Noticing the differences between fossils and modern forms of animals, Lamarck became convinced that plant

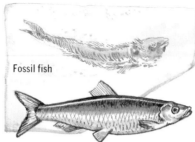

Fossil fish

Living fish

and animal species were not fixed forever, but could change from one generation to the next. His ideas were influenced not only by fossils but also by other geological evidence that suggested that the earth's surface had changed over many years (see page 26).

The Jardin du Roi in Paris where Lamark studied

Lamarck concluded that within their own lifetimes, animals' characteristics could alter in order to cope with their surroundings. He suggested that these changes were then passed on to their offspring. For instance, he argued that the neck of the giraffe would become longer during its lifetime as a result of stretching for leaves in trees, and that this change would then be passed on to the next generation.

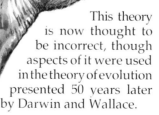

This theory is now thought to be incorrect, though aspects of it were used in the theory of evolution presented 50 years later by Darwin and Wallace.

A South American expedition

Charles Darwin was born in Shrewsbury in England, the son of a successful doctor. He attended school in Shrewsbury and went on to study medicine at the University of Edinburgh. But he did not enjoy the subject and, at his father's insistence, moved to Cambridge University to study for the priesthood. But although he managed to gain a degree, again he was unhappy with the

Charles Darwin (1809-82)

subject. However he showed a great interest in botany and entomology (the study of insects). In 1831 a professor of botany called John Henslow noticed his abilities and found him a place as the naturalist on an expedition to South America. Before leaving, Darwin read works by the geologist Charles Lyell (see page 27). These books made a great impression on him and later influenced his own work.

A page from one of Darwin's notebooks

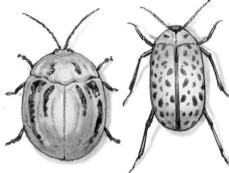

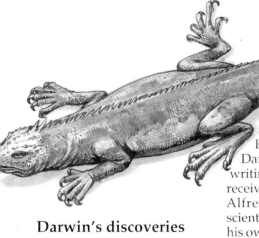

One of the two types of iguana from the Galapagos Islands

Darwin's discoveries

The expedition left in a ship called HMS *Beagle* and was away for five years. During that time it visited Brazil, Argentina, Chile, Peru and the Galapagos Islands, ten rocky islands lying off the coast of Ecuador in the Pacific Ocean, each with different wildlife.

Darwin's drawing of types of finch from the Galapagos Islands

Along the way Darwin built up a huge collection of rocks and fossils as well as samples of plants, birds and animals. He also made very detailed notes of everything he saw on the journey. He later used much of this material, particularly the observations he made on the Galapagos Islands, in the formulation of his theory of evolution.

Beetles collected by Darwin on the expedition

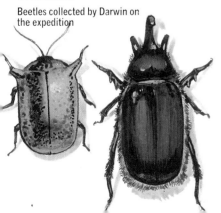

The *Beagle* returned to England in October 1836. Darwin spent the next 20 years writing up his findings. In 1858 he received a manuscript written by Alfred Wallace (1823-1913), a scientist with very similar ideas to his own. Although they presented their ideas together, Darwin's role was seen as more important than Wallace's.

In 1859 Darwin published *On the Origin of the Species by Means of Natural Selection*, which set out his theories on evolution. The book was an immediate success. But it also led to an uproar because it challenged traditional beliefs on the beginning of life on earth. One of the most revolutionary ideas was that all living things had evolved over many millions of years. This rejected the biblical teaching that the world was created in six days and had remained unchanged ever since. Today, most scientists accept a form of the Darwinian theory to explain biological change, although the theory is still being modified. Some people, however, still object to Darwin's ideas on religious grounds.

Cartoon mocking Darwin's idea that humans are descended from apes

Natural selection

Darwin realized that organisms have to compete with each other for food and shelter. He noticed that within each species, some individuals are born with features that by chance make them more able to survive than others. Their offspring inherit these features, which gradually become more common. If other individuals do not have the helpful features, they are more likely to die out. So over many generations the entire species adapts to its environment. This process, called natural selection, can be seen in the way the peppered moth adapted to environmental changes in the 19th century.

At first, the moths were silver and blended with light tree trunks. But as trees became blackened with pollution, the moths were more visible, and so more likely to be eaten by birds. Some individuals, born slightly darker than the others, were less visible and so survived better. They passed on their darker shading to their offspring, and so the entire species became darker.

Silver peppered moth

Black peppered moths blended into the darker background.

The growth of modern chemistry

Chemistry (the study of the substances that make up the world around us) has its origins in the ancient practice of alchemy (see page 10). But alchemy was closely connected to magic and superstition, and is not currently regarded as a true science. Chemistry also has its roots in industrial processes such as iron-working and the making of drugs for medicine. With the growth of experiment and research, the practice of chemistry devloped into a modern science.

An experiment in a 16th-century laboratory

Studying chemical reactions

In 1756 a Scottish experimenter called Joseph Black (1728-99) made an important study of a chemical reaction (the change that takes place when a new substance is formed). Black discovered that when he heated a substance called magnesium carbonate it lost weight. He then suggested that this was because the substance gave off a gas during the heating process. He named the gas "fixed air"; today we know it as carbon dioxide.

A newly discovered gas

Joseph Priestley was born in Yorkshire, England. He trained as a Church minister but soon became interested in scientific research. His work made him famous, but political pressures forced him to leave England for the USA in 1791. In 1774 Priestley made his most important discovery. He noticed that when he heated a chemical called mercuric oxide, a gas was given off. When he placed a lighted candle in the gas, he saw that the flame burned very brightly. At this time, many scientists believed that when something burned it lost a substance they called phlogiston (from *phlox*, the Greek for "flame"). Priestley called his gas "dephlogisticated air" because it seemed to have lost phlogiston. But in fact he had identified the gas we now know as oxygen.

Joseph Priestley (1733-1804)

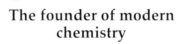

A late 18th-century cartoon of "Doctor Phlogiston"

The founder of modern chemistry

Antoine Lavoisier (1743-94) was born in Paris. He trained as a lawyer but became interested in science and worked as a tax collector in order to support his scientific research. Tax collectors were very unpopular with the leaders of the French Revolution and Lavoisier was one of many people to be executed at the end of the revolution.

Arrest of Lavoisier by French revolutionaries

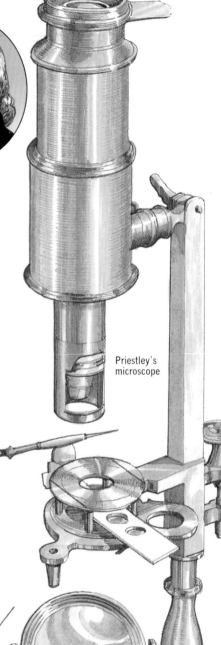

Priestley's microscope

Dalton's symbols of atoms of different elements

The naming of oxygen

Lavoisier performed a series of experiments designed to examine the process of combustion (burning). He heated a number of different substances in air, carefully weighing them before and after heating. His results showed that, rather than losing weight, the substances often became heavier. He reasoned that they must therefore have absorbed something from the air. He showed that this unknown substance was the same gas as the one that Priestley had identified, and renamed it oxygen.

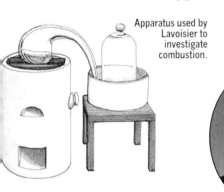

Apparatus used by Lavoisier to investigate combustion.

By successfully explaining some of the phenomena scientists had observed, Lavoisier's results helped to disprove the phlogiston theory, which had been held for nearly a hundred years. His definition of burning - as the uniting of a substance with oxygen - is still used today. He was the first person to demonstrate that all kinds of burning (including the breathing of animals and plants) involve the addition of oxygen. His work helped to overthrow many of the incorrect ideas inherited from alchemy.

Chemical building blocks

In 1789 Lavoisier published *Methods of Chemical Nomenclature*, which built on the work of Robert Boyle (see page 23). In it he developed the idea of elements (substances that cannot be split into simpler substances) as chemical building blocks. Lavoisier listed 33 elements, arranged to show how they combine to form compounds (substances made of more than one element). The book also introduced a new system of naming substances based on their chemical content. Before, they had often had confusing names, some derived from alchemy.

A modern atomic theory

John Dalton was born in a small village in the north of England and taught himself science. His ideas led to a greater understanding of the most fundamental chemical process: the way elements combine to form compounds. In 1808 he published a book called *A New System of Chemical Philosophy*. It had two main points. One was that all chemical elements are composed of very small particles called atoms, which do not break up during chemical reactions. The other was

John Dalton (1766-1844)

that all chemical reactions are the result of atoms joining together or separating. Another important feature of the book was its proposal that different atoms weigh different amounts.

The relationship between elements

Dmitri Mendeleev was born and brought up in Siberia in Russia, the last in a family of 14 children. He was a brilliant student of science at the University of St Petersburg and later became professor of chemistry there. He studied the relationship between different chemical elements. At this time, a few scientists had noticed that some elements had similarities that related to their atomic weights. The atomic weight of an element is the weight of one of its atoms compared with the weight of a hydrogen atom.

Dmitri Mendeleev (1834-1907) and part of his Periodic Table

In 1869 Mendeleev published his Periodic Table of Elements. This grouped the elements into "families" according to their atomic weights, the smallest (hydrogen) on the left, and the largest (lead) on the right. It showed how the elements are related to each other. Mendeleev identified gaps in the periodic table which he claimed represented elements still to be discovered. He was right. Four years later, the first of these, gallium, was discovered. Over a hundred elements have so far been listed.

Some of the equipment used by Dalton

Studying electricity

Electricity plays a very important part in our lives. There are two types: static (not moving) and current (moving). People have known about the effects of electricity since ancient times. But until the end of the 18th century, the only kind they knew how to make was static electricity. The study of electricity became very popular, and during the 19th century people gradually learned more about it and its uses.

Early experiments

In 1705 an English scientist called Francis Hauksbee (c.1666-1713) discovered that if he rubbed a glass globe containing a vacuum (an airless space), it flashed with light. The light was caused by electricity and the globe was acting as an electrical generator.

Hauksbee's static electricity generator

Another man, Stephen Gray (1666-1736), devised experiments which showed that electricity could be conducted (transmitted) through a number of different materials. These included the human body.

An early demonstration of static electricity.

He made electricity travel along a string suspended from cords hung on poles in his orchard.

This French playing card of c.1750 shows a demonstration of static electricity.

Storing static electricity

In 1745 a German priest called Ewald von Kleist (c.1700-48) designed an instrument that could collect and store static electricity. It became known as the Leiden jar, after being used and perfected at the University of Leiden. This was a major development in people's knowledge about electricity. The Leiden jar consisted of a glass jar held in one hand. The inside glass surface was charged (electrified) with static electricity by dipping a brass wire connected to a generator, very similar to Hauksbee's, into the water inside the jar. Once charged, the jar could store the electricity and could also transmit a shock if the wire was touched.

This illustration shows a Leiden jar being charged with static electricity from a generator.

Making electricity useful

One of the first people to study electricity in detail was Benjamin Franklin. He was born in the USA, one of 17 children of a Boston candlemaker. During his long life he had several successful careers: as printer, publisher and politician. At the age of 40 he became interested in electricity, which at that time was mainly used as a form of entertainment in displays. In 1752 Franklin showed that lightning was a form of electricity. He flew a kite fitted with a metal key into a storm cloud. When lightning hit the key, sparks flew off it.

Benjamin Franklin (1706-90)

This experiment was very dangerous and another scientist was later killed doing the same thing. But with it Franklin was able to prove that storm clouds are charged with static electricity. It also showed that lightning is caused by the discharge of that electricity in the form of a very powerful spark. In the same year he fitted the first lightning conductor to the outside wall of a house. This attracted lightning and carried it safely to the ground, preventing damage to the building.

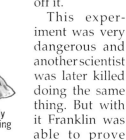

18th-century lady wearing a lightning conductor hat

Animal electricity

Luigi Galvani (1737-98) was professor of anatomy at Bologna University. He realized that an electric ray fish gave a shock similar to that from a Leiden jar. He then wanted to find out whether electricity existed in all forms of life. In 1780, while he was dissecting a dead frog, he noticed that its legs twitched when his scalpel blade touched a nerve. He also noticed that the leg muscles twitched when they were in contact with two different metals, in this case brass and iron. Galvani concluded, mistakenly, that the frog's legs produced electricity and that animals must contain electricity in their muscles and nerves.

Galvani's experiment with frogs' legs

Electricity from metals

Alessandro Volta (1745-1827) showed that the frog's legs did not contain their own form of electricity and that Galvani's results were in fact due to the contact of the two different metals in a damp atmosphere. Using this information, in 1799 Volta succeeded in building the first electric battery. This became known as a "voltaic pile" and was made up of discs of silver and zinc with damp cardboard between them. It generated a steady current of electricity. The volt, a measurement of electricity, is named after him.

The first battery, known as a voltaic pile

Popular science

Michael Faraday was born near London, the son of a blacksmith. His first job was in a bookshop, but in 1813 he started work as a laboratory assistant at the Royal Institution in London. In 1833 he was made professor of chemistry there. Many people now regard Faraday as the greatest of all experimental physicists. He was one of the first people to try to make science popular with the general public. In 1826 he gave the first lectures about science for children, at the Royal Institution. These are still held every year.

Michael Faraday
(1791-1867)

Electricity and magnetism

Faraday became very interested in the relationship between electricity and magnetism. People had known about magnetism for thousands of years, and many believed that electricity and magnetism were related in some way. Then, in 1820, a Danish scientist called Hans Oersted (1777-1851) noticed that a wire with an electric current running through it acted like a magnet, making the needle move on a compass lying nearby.

Investigating this further, Faraday found that when he charged a coil of wire with electricity, an electric current also flowed in another, separate coil nearby. He reasoned that this second current must have been generated by the magnetic effect of the first one.

Faraday argued that if electricity flowing in a wire could produce a magnetic effect, then the opposite might also be true - a magnetic effect should produce an electric current. He found that when he moved a magnet in and out of a coil of wire, the wire became charged with electricity. This showed that magnets alone could produce an electric current and led him to create the first dynamo (a machine that uses mechanical energy to generate electrical energy).

These discoveries had all kinds of far-reaching practical results. Faraday's work led to the invention of the electric motor, and to the development of large-scale systems to generate electricity. This eventually led to the introduction of a public electricity supply.

Faraday produced an electric current by rotating a disc near a magnet, using this device called a disc dynamo.

The fight against disease

During the Renaissance in Europe much progress was made in the understanding of the human body (see page 16). But doctors were still unable to cure a number of diseases, including smallpox and the plague, which killed millions all over the world. Many of these illnesses were caused by viruses (microscopic particles that live off the body's cells). Another problem was that while surgical techniques had improved, many people still died from infections they caught during surgery. From the mid-18th century, scientists began to find ways to beat these forms of disease.

This engraving of 1656 shows an Italian doctor wearing special clothing to protect him against the plague.

Early vaccination

Edward Jenner was born in Gloucestershire, England. From the age of 13 he went to work as an apprentice to a surgeon, and then became a medical student at St George's Hospital, London. After two years Jenner returned to his home town and set up a medical practice. At this time smallpox was one of the most serious viral diseases. Jenner had heard that people who had caught a mild disease called cowpox did not catch smallpox. The cowpox had immunized (protected) them against smallpox. In 1796 Jenner scratched some cowpox into the skin of a healthy boy. Two months later he did the same with smallpox. The experiment was a complete success: the boy did not develop smallpox and had therefore become immune to it. Jenner named the process vaccination, from *vacca*, the Latin word for cow. His work was one of the most important advances in medical science ever made. By 1980 there were no more reported cases of smallpox.

Edward Jenner
(1749-1823)

The birth of bacteriology

Louis Pasteur was born near Dijon in eastern France. In 1843 he went to Paris to study chemistry, and in 1854 he was appointed professor of chemistry at the University of Lille. In Lille, Pasteur was asked to find out why alcohols such as wine and beer sometimes turn sour. He discovered that this was caused by germs called bacteria, and that heating the liquid to a certain temperature killed the bacteria but left the liquid unchanged. This process is now known as "pasteurization" and is used to treat milk. Pasteur also showed that the bacteria which cause liquids to go sour and meat to rot exist invisibly all around us. Pasteur's most famous work was on rabies, one of the most horrific diseases that can affect a human being. It causes paralysis and eventually kills the victim. In 1885 he injected a weak solution of rabies germs into a boy who had been bitten and infected by a rabid (rabies-infected) dog. After a series of these injections the boy recovered completely.

Louis Pasteur
(1822-95)

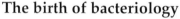

Glass flask and microscope used by Pasteur

A statue of Joseph Meister, the boy Pasteur vaccinated against rabies

Normally the rabies germs would have become active a few weeks after the bite, but this did not happen. The injections, prepared from weakened germs, caused a very mild attack of rabies. This stimulated the boy's resistance, making him immune to the germs from the bite. This is the principle behind all vaccination.

Robert Koch (1843-1910) was, with Pasteur, the founder of the science of bacteriology. Here Koch is inoculating a patient against tuberculosis.

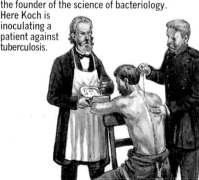

Jenner used these points to scratch vaccine into the skin.

A 19th-century cartoon showing Jenner's patients turning into cows

Antiseptic operations

Joseph Lister was born in Essex, England, the son of a wine merchant and amateur scientist. In 1848 he enrolled at University College, London to study medicine. He qualified in 1852 and, because his work was so outstanding, he was made a Fellow of the Royal College of Surgeons the same year. In 1853 he moved to Edinburgh to take up the post of assistant to James Syme, a leading surgeon. In 1861 Lister was appointed surgeon at the Glasgow Royal Infirmary.

Joseph Lister (1827-1912)

In those days, many patients died after surgical operations. Wounds rarely healed cleanly and usually became septic (badly infected). This often led to blood poisoning and other fatal diseases. In 1865 Pasteur published his theory of germ disease, which claimed that bacteria can cause disease and that fermentation and rotting are caused by bacteria which live in the air. When Lister read this, he thought that the rotting of meat and sepsis of wounds might

These machines sterilize instruments by steam-heating them.

Some modern sterilizing units use ultra-violet light and ultrasound to destroy germs.

be caused by the same thing. Shortly after the publication of Pasteur's paper, Lister performed his first operation in which he took care to clean everything that came into contact with the patient's wound with carbolic acid. This method is known as antisepsis and it destroys germs already present.

As a result of these precautions, the wounds in this and other similar operations healed properly, and the rate of infection fell dramatically. Lister received many awards for his work. His introduction of anti-sepsis to hospitals was one of the major advances in medicine in the 19th century. It changed general surgery from being highly dangerous into something that saves lives.

Lister's antiseptic carbolic spray

This illustration shows Lister directing an antiseptic surgical operation.

Antibiotic drugs

Alexander Fleming was born in Ayrshire, Scotland. From 1901 he studied medicine at St Mary's Hospital, London. Much later, in 1928, when he was studying the bacteria responsible for blood poisoning, he noticed that a dish of the bacteria had become infected

with a growth called *Penicillium notatum*. The bacteria in the area infected by the growth had been killed. The chemical that had caused this is now known as "penicillin".

Alexander Fleming (1881-1955)

Some years later two scientists called Howard Florey (1898-1968) and Ernst Chain (1906-79) produced the first large quantities of purified penicillin. This was the first of a group of drugs called antibiotics which attack and kill bacteria. Because of the development of antibiotics in the 20th century, bacterial illnesses are no longer a major cause of death.

A dish of *Penicillium notatum*, from which penicillin is made

More obstacles

Though smallpox and other diseases have been eradicated, many more fatal diseases still remain. Scientists are still seeking cures for viral and other diseases. Two of the major ones facing doctors today are cancer and the AIDS virus.

Waves and radiation

People have always been interested in nature and the world about them. From the earliest times they asked questions about why things get hot, how light works and sounds are made. Some of these questions were answered by scholars in the ancient world, but in the 19th century scientists began to study problems like these in more detail. They started to describe light, electricity, and magnetism as the products of different kinds of energy.

Developing Faraday's work

James Maxwell was born and brought up near Edinburgh, Scotland. He was a mathematician and physicist whose most important work was on electricity and magnetism. In 1820 Hans Oersted (see page 33) had shown that an electric current had a magnetic effect on a compass needle. An effect like this is now said to be "electromagnetic". Later, Michael Faraday (see page 33) suggested that electric and magnetic forces spread out in "fields" from their sources.

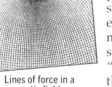

Lines of force in a magnetic field

In 1855 Maxwell developed Faraday's ideas to give a mathematical explanation for the transmission of electromagnetic forces. He devised mathematical equations which showed that the magnetic

James Maxwell (1831-79), with a page of his calculations

field generated by an electric current spreads outward from its source at a constant speed. He calculated that this speed was roughly the same as the speed of light. He suggested that light must therefore be some kind of electromagnetic wave and that the light we can see may be only one of many types of electromagnetic radiation. (Radiation is the emission of rays from a source.)

Radio waves

Heinrich Hertz was born in Hamburg, Germany. He orginally trained to be an engineer but then began studying physics. His experiments showed that electro-magnetic waves emitted by an electrical spark on one side of his laboratory could be detected by a loop of wire

Heinrich Hertz (1857-94)

some distance away. This proved the existence of radio waves, another form of electromagnetic radiation. It was later shown that, like light, radio waves could be focused and reflected. Hertz's work therefore proved Maxwell's earlier theory that electromagnetic waves behave in the same way as light waves.

More electromagnetic waves

Wilhelm Röntgen was born in a small village in Germany and studied at Zürich Polytechnic. He became professor of physics at the University of Würzburg where he experimented with gases and expanded Maxwell's work on electromagnetism.

In 1895 Röntgen was researching cathode rays, which are produced

when an electric current is passed through a glass tube containing a near-vacuum. The tube glows whenever the rays hit the glass. In order to examine this more closely, Röntgen surrounded the tube with a piece of black paper. He was mystified when some cardboard on the other side

Wilhelm Röntgen (1845-1923)

of the room started to glow. It was coated with a chemical, known as a fluorescent, which glows when exposed to light.

Röntgen found that the cardboard still glowed even when he moved it into the next room. It appeared that the tube was emitting another form of radiation which was able to pass through all sorts of materials. He named the new rays X-rays, because of their unknown origin.

An early cathode ray tube

Later Röntgen found that by directing X-rays at a person's hand he could take photographs which showed the bones inside it. The X-rays were stopped by the bones, but passed through the flesh, allowing a photographic image to form.

A 19th-century cartoon of the X-ray effect

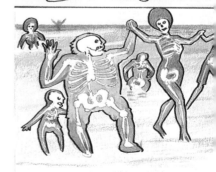

STRAND-IDYLL Á

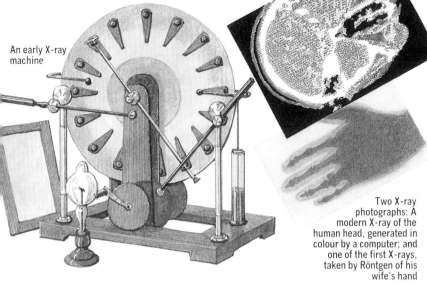

An early X-ray machine

Two X-ray photographs: A modern X-ray of the human head, generated in colour by a computer; and one of the first X-rays, taken by Röntgen of his wife's hand

This revolutionized the medical world, particularly the diagnosis and treatment of broken bones.

The beginning of the atomic era

Antoine Becquerel was born into a scientific family and brought up in Paris. He was a physicist who specialized in the study of fluorescence. When he heard of Röntgen's discovery, he wanted to devise an experiment to find out whether fluorescent chemicals, as well as emitting ordinary light rays, would emit X-rays.

Antoine Becquerel (1852-1908)

At that time Becquerel was studying a fluorescent compound that included an element called uranium. He wrapped some of it in metal foil, then placed the parcel on a photographic plate. He reasoned that any ordinary light emitted by the fluorescence in the substance would not be able to pass through the foil and register on the plate, but that X-rays might. When he developed the plate, it had indeed been blackened, so he was able to confirm that the substance was giving out some type of ray. He later discovered that this only happened with uranium compounds, not with other types of fluorescent chemical.

Becquerel realized that the substance was giving out an extremely strong form of radiation. At first he thought he had found a new form of electromagnetism. But further experiments showed that there were two distinct types of radiation, now known as alpha and beta radiation. These consisted of electrically-charged particles. Later a third type, gamma radiation, was discovered, which was proved to be a form of electromagnetic radiation. These discoveries implied that atoms of radioactive substances were themselves the source of energy. They led scientists to conclude that atoms must therefore have some kind of internal structure that was able to generate this energy. This realization was a very important step, because it marked the beginning of the modern understanding of the atom.

Confirmation of radioactivity

Marya Sklodowska (later Marie Curie) was born in Warsaw, Poland. She left to study chemistry at the Sorbonne in Paris. In 1894 she married another chemist, Pierre Curie (1859-1906).

In their own research into radiation, the Curies discovered that pitchblende, a mineral that contains uranium, is four times as radioactive as pure uranium. They thought that it must therefore contain some other, unknown, radioactive element. The Curies spent several years purifying huge quantities of pitchblende, which became increasingly radioactive. By 1902 they had gathered 0.1 gram of the unknown element, which they gave the name "radium".

Caricature of the Curies

In 1903 the Curies received the Nobel Prize for physics. When Pierre was killed in a car crash three years later, Marie took over as professor in Paris, the first woman to hold such a position. In 1911 she was awarded the Nobel Prize for chemistry, the first person to receive two Nobel prizes.

Radium, used in small doses, became very important in the treatment of cancer. But years of exposure to it damaged Curie's own health, and she died of a blood cancer called leukemia.

A medal of Marie Curie (1867-1934), issued on the centenary of her birth

The science of life

Although by the end of the 19th century Darwin's theory of evolution was accepted by many scientists, there were a few who disagreed with it. They claimed that it did not explain how changes originated in plants and animals, or how characteristics were passed on from one generation to the next. People began to investigate these questions. Their studies led to the foundation of genetics, the science of heredity (how characteristics in plants and animals are inherited).

The birth of genetics

Gregor Mendel grew up in Heinzendorf in Austria. He became a priest at the monastery in Brno in 1847, and was elected abbot there eleven years later.

Mendel was interested in how plants pass on particular features such as height and shape to their offspring. He bred pea plants to find out how this worked, and noticed that characteristics like the shape of their flowers were passed on to the next generation. He also found that some features were more likely to be inherited than others. Those that had a three in four chance of being inherited he called "dominant". Those that only had a one in four chance of being inherited he called "recessive".

Mendel suggested that each characteristic was controlled by a pair of units (now called genes), one from each parent. This is known as Mendel's First

Mendel performed most of his experiments on pea plants.

Law. His discoveries and theories revealed the secret of heredity and formed the basis of modern studies in genetics. However, though he published his work in 1866, its true significance remained unrecognized for nearly forty years.

Gregor Mendel (1822-84)

Experiments with fruit flies

Thomas Morgan (1866-1945) was born in Kentucky, USA. He founded the department of biology at the California Institute of Technology in 1928, and ran it for the rest of his life. At first Morgan was one of the fiercest critics of Mendel's theory of heredity, but he later became its strongest supporter. He wanted to find out whether the kind of changes Mendel had noticed in plants also occurred in animals. In 1908 he began studying fruit flies; this work was very important in establishing Mendel's theories.

Fruit flies normally have red eyes, but Morgan found a white-eyed male in one of the breeding jars. When he bred this male with other members of the same generation, some white-eyed flies appeared again in

Fruit flies (Drosophila melanogaster)

the next generation. They were mostly male, but when one of these white-eyed males mated with females of the first generation, half the males and half the females of their offspring had white eyes. Morgan used Mendel's theory to explain this result by showing that the dominant feature of white eyes was passed on by the male parent's units.

Mapping chromosomes

All organisms (living things) are made up of cells, the basic units of life. Inside each cell is a tiny ball called a nucleus, which in turn contains thread-like forms called chromosomes.

Morgan and his research team discovered that the units suggested by Mendel were indeed actual physical units, placed at definite positions along each chromosome. They named the units "genes", after the Greek word for birth. Using this discovery, they were able to work out the first "chromo-some map". This showed the position of the genes on a chromosome. By 1922 they had worked out a map

Magnified human chromosomes

showing the positions of more than 2000 genes on the chromosomes of fruit flies. This enabled them to identify the gene responsible for the white eyes in the flies. In this way they confirmed that Mendel's theories were correct, and provided the evidence to explain them.

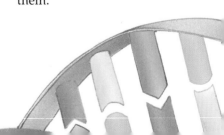

Molecular biology

Genes provide a chemical code of instructions to control the way plants and animals look and how their bodies work. A "copy" of these instructions is passed from parents to their offspring. The study of how this happens is part of an important area of scientific research known as molecular biology, which is concerned with the structure of the molecules that make up living animals and plants.

Cross-section of an animal cell, magnified many times

Cell membrane (outer skin)

Nucleus

By the early 20th century scientists knew that plant and animal cells contained a chemical called deoxyribonucleic acid (DNA). By 1950, they thought that DNA molecules acted as the chemical code of instructions responsible for heredity, but they did not know what they looked like or how they worked. A number of scientists were using a variety of approaches to solve the problem.

Building the DNA model

Francis Crick was brought up in London. He studied physics at the University of London and then biology at Cambridge University.

With an American scientist called James Watson (b.1928), he carried out research into the structure of DNA. They also used the results of the work of other scientists, in particular Maurice Wilkins (b.1916) and Rosalind Franklin. Wilkins and Franklin studied DNA using X-ray photographs. Their work was crucial in the eventual discovery of the structure of DNA and how it transmits genetic information from one generation to the following one.

Francis Crick (b.1916)

In 1953, Crick and Watson built a scale model of the DNA molecule from pieces of wire and plastic balls. Its shape was that of a double helix, which looks like a twisted rope ladder. It showed how the DNA molecule divides to form two identical copies of itself.

Rosalind Franklin (1920-58)

When plants and animals reproduce, each of the cells they are made up from divides into two copies. Every time a new cell is

This is a computer-generated illustration showing the structure of the DNA molecule.

made, the DNA is also copied, so that when the cell divides, each of the two new cells has its own copy of the instructions responsible for heredity. In this way the characteristics are passed from parents to their offspring.

Many scientists regard this as one of the most important discoveries of the 20th century. In 1962 Crick, Watson and Wilkins were awarded the Nobel Prize for Medicine. Had she not died very young from cancer, Rosalind Franklin would have shared the prize with them.

1. DNA consists of two strands shaped in a double helix, like a twisted rope ladder.

5. Two new identical strands are formed

2. The steps in the ladder are made up of four chemical building blocks, called bases, which are linked in pairs.

3. The two DNA strands separate

4. Spare bases join their matching pairs on the separated strands.

Opening up the atom

At the end of the 19th century, many physicists believed they were close to explaining the construction of the universe. They described matter in terms of the movement of tiny, indivisible particles called atoms. However, new discoveries threatened their confidence. It became apparent that atoms themselves were composed of even smaller particles, and that the way in which they behaved could not be explained by Newton's laws of force and motion (see page 22).

The birth of quantum physics

Max Planck was born in Kiel, now in Germany. He studied physics at Munich University, where he later became a professor. In 1900 he published an article introducing the idea of "quantizing energy". On the basis of Planck's work, Einstein suggested that electromagnetic radiation (see page 36), instead of being made up of waves, is in fact discontinuous and is composed of tiny particles, or "quanta", of energy.

Max Planck
(1858-1947)

This equation, formulated by Einstein, includes Planck's constant (h). This relates the mechanical properties of matter to its wave properties.

Although Planck's idea was not seen as revolutionary at the time, it led to the development of quantum mechanics, a new set of laws describing how atomic particles behaved. Unlike Newton's laws, quantum mechanics is based on the idea that matter can behave either as waves or as particles.

From clerk to professor

Albert Einstein is one of the 20th century's most famous scientists. But he was a shy man whose work was very abstract and theoretical. He is best known for his relativity theories and for establishing the idea of the quantization of energy, both of which are important for describing how atoms and atomic particles move and interact.

Einstein was born in Ulm, Germany. His family moved to Switzerland and he studied physics at Zürich Polytechnic. After failing to secure an academic position, he became a clerk in Berne.

In 1905, Einstein worked in his spare time to produce three papers which re-examined some of the most fundamental ideas in science. His theories were so revolutionary that they were not immediately accepted, but his ability was quickly recognized. In 1909 he became a professor at Zürich University, and then in 1914 moved to the University of Berlin.

Albert Einstein
(1879-1955)

The University of Berlin

The relativity theories

The first paper on relativity (known as the Special Theory of Relativity) overturned Newton's view of fixed measurements of time and motion. Einstein showed that all movement is relative; that all we can measure is how fast we are moving in relation to something else. There is a relation between the mass and energy of moving objects, which he expressed in the equation $E=mc^2$. This means that the energy (E) contained in any particle of matter is equal to its mass (m) multiplied by the square of the speed of light (c^2). This formula is at the heart of all methods of obtaining nuclear energy.

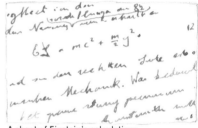

A sheet of Einstein's calculations

In 1915 Einstein published a second paper on relativity (the General Theory of Relativity), which dealt with what happens when an object is speeding up or slowing down. It included the idea that light has mass and is therefore affected by gravity. This theory was confirmed when the bending of light by gravity was detected by photographing the light from two stars during a solar eclipse in 1919. Einstein's discoveries caused a sensation and made him internationally famous.

A computer image of a solar eclipse

The heart of the atom

Ernest Rutherford is important for his brilliant experimental and theoretical work on the nucleus (core) of the atom, and for his laboratory skills. The son of a New Zealand farmer, Rutherford studied at Christchurch College where he carried out research based on Hertz's study of radio waves (see page 36). He won a scholarship to Cambridge University, England and worked at the Cavendish Laboratory on the recently discovered X-rays and uranium radiation (see page 37).

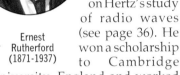

Ernest Rutherford (1871-1937)

Autunite, an ore from which uranium can be extracted

Rutherford was appointed a professor at McGill University in Montreal, and later returned to Britain as director of the Manchester physics laboratory. He and his team carried out important experiments into the structure of the atom, using particles called

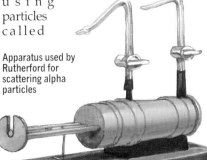

Apparatus used by Rutherford for scattering alpha particles

alpha particles, which are emitted by radioactive substances.

From his experiments, Rutherford built up a detailed picture of the atom. He concluded that most atomic matter was concentrated into a tiny nucleus in the middle, with much lighter particles called electrons orbiting it, like planets around the sun. In 1908 Rutherford was awarded the Nobel Prize for Chemistry, and in 1919 he was appointed director of the Cavendish Laboratory, where he inspired much further research into atomic structure.

A new model of the atom

Niels Bohr grew up in Copenhagen, Denmark, the son of a professor of physiology. He was awarded a doctorate from Copenhagen University and in 1911 moved to Manchester to work with Rutherford. By 1913 he had devised a radical new model of the structure of the atom. It combined Rutherford's ideas with those of quantum mechanics. Bohr's model has now been superseded, but it is still a useful aid to understanding

the way atoms behave.

In 1913 Bohr returned to Copenhagen as professor of physics and helped develop new theories of quantum mechanics. He drew up models of the structure of the nucleus and discussed the energy changes involved in nuclear fission. He won the Nobel Prize for Physics in 1922.

Niels Bohr (1885-1962)

Bohr was a committed anti-fascist and, when the Germans invaded Denmark in 1940, he refused to participate in atomic research for the Nazis. In 1943, in danger of arrest, he escaped by boat to Sweden and then on to the United States.

This diagram is based on Bohr's work into the structure of the atom. He showed that electrons move around the nucleus in defined energy levels, sometimes called shells.

Shells

Nucleus

Electron

The origin of the universe

For thousands of years people have been seeking answers to questions about the origin of the universe. For a long time many people thought that the universe had always existed in its present form, and that it would always remain the same. But ideas on the nature of the universe have altered as scientific understanding has increased. Evidence gathered over the centuries has shown that, rather than staying the same, the universe is always changing. The science of the universe is called cosmology. Cosmologists study the entire universe to find out how it began and how it has evolved.

View of the Andromeda Spiral

thought that our galaxy, known as the Milky Way, made up the entire universe. They believed that the spiral forms we now know to be other galaxies were only clouds of gases. But Hubble saw stars on the edge of the Andromeda Spiral and estimated that they lay well beyond the Milky Way. His work proved that the Andromeda Spiral was another galaxy and therefore that other galaxies existed apart from our own. Gradually he and others began to identify more galaxies.

wavelength increases. The greater the speed at which the light source is moving away, the greater the red shift. Hubble realized that in order to produce the shift effect, the stars must be moving away from us. He also noticed that the fainter the galaxies were, the greater the red shift. This implied that the more distant the galaxies

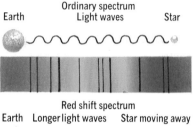

Ordinary spectrum

Earth — Light waves — Star

Red shift spectrum

Earth — Longer light waves — Star moving away

were, the faster they were moving. By 1929 he was able to measure the degree of red shift to calculate the speed of the galaxies and their distance from the earth. He found that the speed increases in proportion to the distance. This is known as Hubble's Law. His work provided the first evidence that the universe is expanding. This is the key to the Big Bang theory (see below). In addition, once astronomers were able to measure the speed at which galaxies are moving outward, they could calculate when the universe began. They now believe this happened between six and fifteen billion years ago.

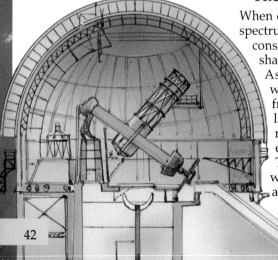

This bronze plate depicts the Chinese idea of the creation of the universe.

Galaxies beyond our own

Edwin Hubble was born and brought up in the USA and studied law at the University of Chicago. He first worked as a lawyer but then turned to astronomy. For the rest of his life he worked at Mount Wilson Observatory in California.

In 1923 Hubble examined a galaxy (a giant group of stars) called the Andromeda Spiral. At that time, most astronomers
The Mount Wilson Observatory

This picture shows Edwin Hubble (1889-1953) at the controls of the Mount Wilson telescope.

The age of the universe

When examined closely, the light spectrum (see page 22) not only consists of the range of different shades, but also a series of lines. Astronomers noticed that when they examined light from stars, the shades and lines had moved toward the red end of the spectrum. This effect is known as "red shift". The reason for this is that when a source of light moves away from an observer, its

Creation from explosion

Georges Lemaître was born in Belgium. He studied astronomy at the University of Louvain in Belgium and then trained as a priest. He moved to Cambridge University in England and was later appointed professor of astronomy at Louvain where he remained for the rest of his career.

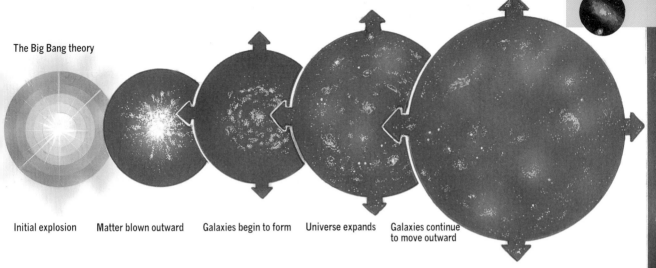

The Big Bang theory

Initial explosion | Matter blown outward | Galaxies begin to form | Universe expands | Galaxies continue to move outward

In 1927, using Einstein's General Theory of Relativity (see page 40), Lemaître proposed that the universe was still expanding. He claimed that at one time it must have been compressed into a tiny atom of energy and matter. He went on to suggest that the atom blew apart in a huge explosion, scattering hot gases in all directions This idea has become known as the Big Bang theory. At the time its true importance was not fully appreciated, but most scientists now see it as the best explanation of the origin of the universe.

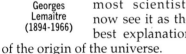

Georges Lemaître (1894-1966)

As new discoveries in space have been made, the Big Bang theory has been refined and modified. In 1970 Roger Penrose (b.1931) and Stephen Hawking (b.1942) proved that if Einstein's General Theory of Relativity is correct, then it is possible that there was a definite beginning to the universe. At this point, called a singularity, space and time as we know them would not have existed. Moments after the explosion, the universe would have been an incredibly hot fireball. It expanded and cooled until, millions of years later, hydrogen and then other elements formed. Eventually, gravity drew atoms together and galaxies began to develop.

Another modification of the Big Bang theory, called the Oscillating Universe theory, states that the universe is alternately expanding and contracting. If this is true, when the limit of expansion is reached, the growth will stop and gravity will pull everything back together

The Oscillating Universe theory

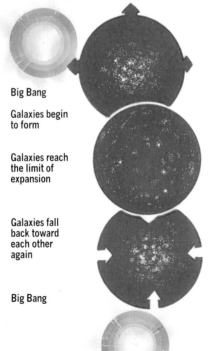

Big Bang

Galaxies begin to form

Galaxies reach the limit of expansion

Galaxies fall back toward each other again

Big Bang

once more. The galaxies will be squeezed together so tightly that another cosmic explosion will set the whole process off again.

Staying the same

Hermann Bondi grew up in Vienna, Austria. He moved to England and studied at Cambridge University. In 1954 he became professor of mathematics at King's College London.

In 1948 Bondi proposed the Steady State theory, which says that new galaxies form in the middle of the expanding universe to replace those moving outward. As a result, he claimed, the universe would always look the same. However, later findings contradict this. For example, in 1964 two astronomers called Robert Wilson and Arno Penzias picked up faint radio noise from space. This is now thought to be the echo of the Big Bang.

Hermann Bondi (b.1919)

Wilson (b.1936) and Penzias (b.1933)

Women in science

Although many women throughout history have been involved in the development of science, their work has gained little recognition. For a number of reasons their achievements have often been ignored and their names left out of books. Women were unable to attend universities and were excluded from scientific societies and laboratories. Because they had little scientific education, many women could only serve as assistants to male scientists. The situation has improved slowly, but there are still far fewer women working in the sciences than there are men.

Early women scientists

Although there were women doctors in Ancient Egypt and Greece, there were very few opportunities for women to work in medicine and science in the ancient world. Accounts of the lives of successful women were invariably written by men who dismissed women scientists as immoral and dangerous. The first such scientist whose life is well-documented is Hypatia. Most of her writings have been lost, but there are a number of references to them by other scientists. Hypatia was born in Alexandria in Egypt, where she taught mathematics and philosophy. Her most important work was in algebra and geometry, but she was also interested in mechanics and technology. In

Tombstone of a woman doctor from the 1st century A.D.

Hypatia of Alexandria (A.D.370-415), based on a classical statue

addition she designed several scientific instruments, including a plane astrolabe. This was used for measuring the positions of the stars, planets and the sun.

Abbess and physician

Hildegard of Bingen was the abbess of a convent in Germany. She was educated in a wide range of subjects, including music and medicine. She wrote many books on religion as well as a natural history encyclopaedia called *Liber simplicis medicinae* which described animals and minerals and as many as 230 plants and 60 trees. Hildegard devised a number of maps of the universe. In her first plan (shown below) of the universe, the earth lies in the middle surrounded by the stars and planets.

Hildegard of Bingen (1098-1179)

Hildegard's first plan of the universe

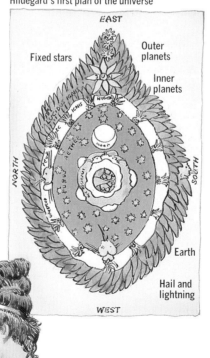

EAST

Fixed stars

Outer planets

Inner planets

NORTH

SOUTH

Earth

Hail and lightning

WEST

A forgotten mathematician

Anne, Countess of Conway (1631-79), a mathematician and philosopher, was born in London. Her brother, who acted as her tutor, supplied her with books and introduced her to the ideas of Descartes (see page 19). Her country house became a well-known meeting place for scholars.

Ragley Hall, Lady Anne Conway's country house

Anne Conway's book, *The Principles of the most Ancient and Modern Philosophy*, was published eleven years after her death by a Dutch chemist called Francis van Helmont. It contained many of her scientific ideas and had a great influence on a German mathematician called Gottfried Leibniz (1646-1716). Although Leibniz acknowledged her importance, Conway's work was attributed to van Helmont and her name was soon forgotten.

A self-taught astronomer

Caroline Herschel (1750-1848) was born into a family of German musicians. In 1772 she moved to England to join her brother William, an astronomer. After teaching herself astronomy and mathematics with his help, she became his assistant. Later, in 1787, she became the first woman to be appointed assistant to the Court Astronomer.

This giant telescope, designed by Caroline's brother William, was built about 1780.

Finding new comets

Herschel became recognized throughout Europe as a great astronomer. As well as her important collaborations with her brother, independently she discovered many new comets. She won a number of awards for her work, including the Gold Medal of the Royal Astronomical Society in 1828. Her success helped to open up astronomy to other women of her time.

Spreading scientific ideas

Mary Somerville made important contributions to science education. Born in Scotland, she became known as "the Queen of 19th-century science". Her first scientific paper, *On the Magnetizing Power of the More Refrangible Solar Rays*, had to be submitted to the Royal Society by her husband because women were banned from the organization. In 1831 she published *Mechanism of the Heavens*. As well as being her interpretation of the work of a French scientist called Pierre de Laplace (1749-1827), the book contained many original ideas of her own. For the rest of the century it was a standard text in the study of advanced mathematics.

Mary Somerville (1780-1872) and the title page of *Mechanism of the Heavens*

The first computer programmer

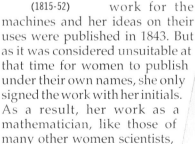

Ada, Countess of Lovelace, daughter of the poet Lord Byron, studied astronomy, Latin, music and mathematics. She worked with an English mathematician called Charles Babbage (1792-1871), as the designer of arithmetical operations for his calculating machines. As these machines are now often seen as the forerunners of computers, in a sense Lovelace was the first computer programmer. Her work for the machines and her ideas on their uses were published in 1843. But as it was considered unsuitable at that time for women to publish under their own names, she only signed the work with her initials. As a result, her work as a mathematician, like those of many other women scientists, has been largely forgotten.

Countess of Lovelace (1815-52)

Academic frustration

Sophia Krukovsky was a Russian mathematician who gained the very highest awards for her work but was continually blocked in her efforts to make a career in mathematics. After her marriage to a law student called Vladimir Kovalevsky, she moved with him to Heidelberg in Germany. As a woman, Krukovsky was not allowed to join the university there and had to study privately. In 1874 she was awarded a doctorate in mathematics from Göttingen University, but was unable to find an academic post.

Sophia Krukovsky (1850-91) and some of her mathematical calculations

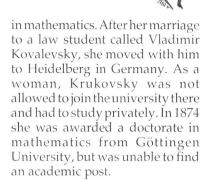

In 1884 Krukovsky became the first woman professor at the new University of Stockholm, Sweden. In 1888 she was awarded the Prix Bordin, the highest prize of the French Académie des Sciences (part of the Institute de France; see page 21) for her work in mathematics. But still she was unable to secure a job in France. She decided to resign her post at Stockholm and to devote her time to research, but she became ill and died soon after.

The letter announcing Krukovsky's award of the Prix Bordin.

Key dates in scientific discovery

Dates B.C.

4241B.C.   The first year in which events can be precisely dated. This is made possible by the Egyptian calendar.

c.2630B.C.   Imhotep becomes medical adviser to Djoser, Pharaoh of Egypt.

c.1000B.C.   First records of Chinese knowledge of astronomy.

c.700B.C.   Original compilation of the *Ayurveda*, an ancient Indian medical text.

c.600B.C.   Thales of Miletus tries to find rational explanations for natural phenomena.

551B.C.   Birth of the Chinese philosopher Confucius.

c.500B.C.   Pythagoras discusses the mystical importance of numbers and harmony in the universe.

c.450B.C.   Birth of Hippocrates, later an influential doctor on the island of Cos.

399B.C.   Death of Socrates, one of the most important Greek philosophers.

387B.C.   The philosopher Plato establishes the Academy in Athens.

c.335B.C.   Aristotle writes important scientific books on natural history and the structure of the universe.

287B.C.   Birth of Archimedes, mathematician and inventor.

Dates A.D.

150   Ptolemy writes the *Almagest*, about the movements of the stars and planets.

161   Greek anatomist Galen moves to Rome, where he becomes a famous doctor.

c.600   Mayan civilization flourishes in Central America.

813   The school of astronomy is founded in Baghdad.

c.854   Birth of al-Razi (Rhazes), the greatest Arabic alchemist.

965   Birth of ibn al-Haytham (Alhazen), an Islamic physicist famous for his work on optics.

1253   Death of Robert Grosseteste, teacher of mathematics and science.

1264   Thomas Aquinas reconciles Christian thought with Aristotle's teachings.

1267   Roger Bacon challenges the authority of traditional Christian education.

1452   Birth of Leonardo da Vinci, inventor and artist.

1527   Paracelsus becomes professor of medicine at the university of Basle.

1543   Copernicus publishes his theory that the planets move around the sun, not around the earth.
Andreas Vesalius produces a new guide to human anatomy.

1551   Konrad von Gesner starts to publish his extensive study of the animal kingdom.

1574   Tycho Brahe sets up an astronomical observatory on the island of Hven.

1596   Birth of René Descartes, mathematician and philosopher.

1610   Galileo Galilei publishes *The Starry Messenger*, about his astronomical discoveries made with the use of the telescope.

1616   William Harvey lectures on the circulation of blood.

1618   Johannes Kepler publishes laws describing the planets' elliptical orbits round the sun.

1627   Publication of Francis Bacon's *New Atlantis*, with its influential ideas about the role of science in society.

1632   Galileo publishes *Dialogue Concerning the Two Chief World Systems*, which describes the earth's movement around the sun.

1642   Galileo dies.
Isaac Newton is born.

1644   Publication of Descartes' most important scientific work, *Principles of Philosophy*.

1661   Robert Boyle proposes that matter is made up of tiny corpuscles, in his book *The Sceptical Chymist*.

1662   The Royal Society is founded in London.

1665   Publication of Robert Hooke's *Micrographia*, which contains detailed drawings made with the assistance of microscopes.

1666   The Académie Royale des Sciences is founded in Paris.

1682   Edmond Halley charts and describes the orbit of a comet, which is later named after him.

1687   Publication of Isaac Newton's book *Principia*, in which he formulates his laws of universal gravity.

1703   Newton becomes president of the Royal Society, and retains this post until his death in 1727.

1704   Newton publishes his book *Opticks*, about lenses and light.
John Ray completes his classification of 17,000 plants.

1705   Francis Hauksbee produces flashes of electricity by rubbing a globe containing a vacuum.

1729   Stephen Gray conducts electricity over long distances.

1745   Invention of the Leiden jar, an instrument that stores electricity.

1748   Georges de Buffon completes his 36-volume survey of natural history.

1752   Benjamin Franklin shows that lightning is caused by electricity.

1753 Carl Linnaeus publishes his new binomial system for classifying plants.

1756 Joseph Black finds "fixed air" (carbon dioxide) can be produced by heating chemicals.

1774 Joseph Priestley isolates the gas we now know as oxygen, calling it "dephlogisticated air".

1775 Abraham Werner founds a mining school at Freiberg, and gradually develops the "Neptunist" theory of geological change.

1779 Antoine Lavoisier confirms the existence of "dephlogisticated air", and renames it oxygen.

1787 Caroline Herschel receives royal recognition for her contributions to astronomy.

1789 Publication of Lavoisier's *Methods of Chemical Nomenclature*, which lists 33 elements, and introduces the modern system of naming them.

1791 Luigi Galvani publishes the results of his electrical experiments on frogs.

1795 James Hutton's book *The Theory of the Earth* questions the biblical account of the creation. It suggests instead that geological change has taken place over millions of years.

1796 Edward Jenner vaccinates a child against smallpox.

1799 Alessandro Volta builds the first electric battery.

1808 John Dalton's book *A New System of Chemical Philosophy* contains important new ideas about atomic theory.

1809 Jean de Lamarck publishes his explanation of change in living beings, including his idea that acquired characteristics can be inherited.

1820 Hans Oersted shows that an electric current has a magnetic effect on a compass needle.

1824 Justus von Liebig sets up his research laboratory in Giessen, Germany.

1831 Charles Lyell is appointed professor of geology at King's College, London.
Charles Darwin embarks on his voyage on HMS *Beagle*.
Michael Faraday produces an electric current from a moving magnet.

1843 Ada Lovelace publishes her mathematical work.

1858 Darwin receives Alfred Wallace's manuscript about natural selection.

1859 Darwin publishes *On the Origin of the Species by Natural Selection*, which contains his theories of evolution.

1867 Joseph Lister describes his success in reducing infections by using antiseptics.

1868 Gregor Mendel finishes his research into pea plants, which forms the basis of modern genetic theory.

1869 Dmitri Mendeleev devises the Periodic Table of the Elements.

1871 Darwin publishes his second book on evolution, *The Descent of Man*.

1872 James Maxwell uses algebraic equations to quantify Faraday's electrical theories.

1882 Robert Koch discovers the cholera virus.

1885 Using vaccinations, Louis Pasteur saves the life of a boy bitten by a rabid dog.

1886 Heinrich Hertz begins research that demonstrates the existence of radio waves.

1888 Sophia Krukovsky wins the Prix Bordin.

1895 Wilhelm Röntgen discovers X-rays.

1896 Antoine Becquerel discovers that uranium is radioactive.

1900 Max Planck introduces the idea of "quantizing energy".

1905 Albert Einstein publishes three scientific papers, including the Special Theory of Relativity.

1910 Thomas Morgan's experiments with fruit flies confirm Mendel's ideas about heredity.

1911 Marie Curie receives the Nobel Prize for her work on radioactivity, becoming the first person to win the prize twice.
Ernest Rutherford shows that atoms have a central nucleus.

1913 Niels Bohr proposes a new model of the hydrogen atom.

1915 Alfred Wegener publishes his theory of continental drift.

1919 Einstein publishes his paper on General Relativity.

1923 Edwin Hubble proves the existence of galaxies beside our own.

1927 Georges Lemaître proposes that the universe is continually expanding.

1928 Alexander Fleming notices that a growth, now called penicillin, kills bacteria.

1929 Hubble shows that the galaxies are moving away from each other. This forms the basis of the Big Bang theory.

1948 Hermann Bondi and Thomas Gold propose the Steady State theory of the universe.

1953 Francis Crick and James Watson discover the structure of the DNA molecule.

1963 Geological experiments confirm Wegener's ideas, and establish the theory of plate tectonics.

1964 Robert Wilson and Arno Penzias detect radio noise from space. This is thought to be the echo of the Big Bang.

Index

The publishers are grateful to the following organizations for permission to reproduce their material, or to use it as artist's reference:

Science Museum Library, London; The Royal Society; The Ann Ronan Picture Library; Popperfoto; Mary Evans Picture Library; Bibliothèque Nationale, Paris; Dover Publications Inc.

The three pictures at the bottom of p.18 are based on drawings by Leonardo da Vinci in the Royal Collection, Windsor.

Universal Edition

First published in 1992 by Usborne Publishing Ltd, 83-85 Saffron Hill, London EC1N 8RT, England.
First published in America March 1993
Copyright © 1992 by Usborne Publishing Ltd. All rights reserved. No part of this publication may be reproduced, stored in a retrieval system, or transmitted in any form, or by any means, electronic, mechanical, photocopying, recording, or otherwise, without prior permission of the publisher.

The name Usborne and the device 🐝 are Trade Marks of Usborne Publishing Ltd. Printed in Spain.